The Lollipop Trollops

Also by Alexander Theroux

NOVELS

Three Wogs
Darconville's Cat
An Adultery

FABLES

The Schinocephalic Waif
The Great Wheadle Tragedy
Master Snickup's Cloak

THE LOLLIPOP TROLLOPS

AND OTHER POEMS BY ALEXANDER THEROUX

DALKEY ARCHIVE PRESS

Acknowledgments

Some of these poems have appeared (often in different form and sometimes under different titles) in *Ariel: The Book of Fantasy, Five Poets, Georgia Review, Graham House Review, Harvard Advocate, Iowa Review, Poetry Bag, Poetry East, Review of Contemporary Fiction, Transatlantic Review,* and in my novel *Darconville's Cat,* to whose editors the author makes grateful acknowledgment.

I would also like to acknowledge, with gratitude, the Lannan Foundation, especially Patrick Lannan and Jim Butler, whose assistance and generosity has helped make this book possible.

Fifteen of these poems appeared in *History Is Made at Night and Other Poems,* a limited edition printed by the Aralia Press in March 1992.

Library of Congress Cataloging-in-Publication Data
Theroux, Alexander.
    The lollipop trollops and other poems / by Alexander Theroux.
    Includes index.
    I. Title.
PS3570.H38L65   1992   811'.54—dc20   92-12510
ISBN 1-56478-006-6 (paperback)
ISBN 1-56478-007-4 (cloth)
ISBN 1-56478-008-2 (limited edition)

First edition

Cover design by Edward Gorey

Partially funded by grants from The National Endowment for the Arts and The Illinois Arts Council.

Dalkey Archive Press
Fairchild Hall/ISU
Normal, IL 61761

Printed on permanent/durable acid-free paper and bound in the United States of America.

to the good soul of my cat,
Rat

Contents

Introduction   xi

Admissions   1
Alexander Theroux   2
Amelia Earhart   3
Andover Spires   5
Anecdote of Santa Fé   6
Are the Skeletons of Fat Men Fat   7
Ars Poetica   9
Assumption   11
Auden's Face   12
A un romancier de ma connaisance qui ne mesure qu' 1m 70   13
Billy the Kid Questions the Dark   14
Black Racist   15
Blackwind at Prayer   16
Boogie Man Blues   17
Boston Irish Pols   18
A Boston Marriage   19
Brahms   21
Bridalveil Falls   22
By the Waters Now of Doom I Sit   23
Café du Télégraphe Anglais   24
Camera Lucida   25
Cat Noises   28
Catharine   29
Chirico by Chirico   30
A Christmas Pome   32
"Circle" Burke   34
Cocaine Cat   35
Cochiti Love   36
Colloquy with Miss Rita Hayworth   37
Communion Tongues   38
Contrasting Fruitage   41
Counterparts   43
Creeping Judas   45
Criminal Man   48
Crow   49
Darconville's Sonnet   50
A Daughter's Confession   51
Deliriants   52
Departmental Secretaries at Yale   53
Emily Dickinson's Bread   54
Everyone's Fat Friend Is First to Coo   55
Février   56
Fiction's Fun to Feign   57

Formal Theater   58
Francesca da Rimini   59
Fr. Mario   60
The Gesture of Vanni Fucci   62
The Girl Who Makes You Cry Is Always Love   63
God   64
The Good Old Song   65
The Harvard College Tinies   68
Harvest Time   70
Haves and Holes   71
History Is Made at Night   73
The Hollywood Rag   74
I Think of Death at Times   75
If Love Is the Licking and Tugs at the Movies   76
Iliad   78
Imagos   79
Insect   80
In the Children's Parks Is Fun   81
Job   82
Joni James   83
La Compagnie idéal   84
Le Bruit   85
Little League Parents   86
The Lollipop Trollops   87
Lost Friend   90
Lost in America   91
Love, 1957   93
Loverboy   94
The Man with the Fenestrate Shoes   95
Mary Snowfire   96
Medford Kids   97
The Meeting of the Heads   98
Megabucks Ticket   99
Mens Sana in Corpore Sano   100
Milagro   101
Mill Stream   102
The Miracle of Fasting   103
Monsieur Trinquet   104
Moses the Lawgiver   105
Mother Gideon   107
Mrs. Mixter   108
Mussolini   109
The Night of the Niffelheim Dwarfs   111
Padre Todopoderoso   113

Part of Loving's Leaving   114
Patriotic Bigots   115
Passacaglia for an Italian Witch   116
Pathology of War   117
Peasant Festival   118
Phantom of Werther   120
Pimp   121
Poem for a Christening   122
A Poem in Which Is a Celebration by Negation   123
Prayer for Manon   124
Provincetown Chat   125
The Raven   126
Reveries of Children Dying   128
Romard   130
Samoan Brother   131
Sarcastic Middle-aged Women   132
Six Limericks   133
Sneezes   134
Snobbish Women at McDonald's   135
The Spittoon Has Gone Ceramic   137
The Star-Spangled Banner   139
Strange in My Hencoop   141
Tammy Wynette   143
Thanks for the Memory   145
Three Questions   147
Tiresias in Mushroom Town   148
To R.J.   149
To the Eight American Women Soldiers Slain in Vietnam   150
Turkana Girl   151
TV News in America   152
Vinyl Junkie   153
The Way to Cedar Rapids   154
Welsh Englyn   156
When the Circumcision Screams Die Down   157
When You're Looking with Your Right Eye   158
Who Isn't What   159
A Widgin of a Thing with a Face Like a Gun   160
Winterreise   161
Winter Wounds   162
Wittgenstein's Proposal   163
The World as Will and Idea   164
Yale   166
Zucchini   167

Index of First Lines   169

Introduction

I am a novelist, although I have written plays, essays, short stories, fables, and now in this particular gathering poems. Many of these poems, in my opinion, are like novels, to tell the truth, in kind if not in degree. There are characters here. And plots. The rainbow of fiction arcs over the many little hills and valleys of these hundred or so poems, at least to me, whether they are narrative or not. Perhaps they are only poems a novelist would write, but to my mind there is little generic difference between poetry and artistic prose. Rhythm can be found in the prose of all great writers, the magic of prosody being often its first flower (phrasing, idiom, intonation), as V. Nabokov, who wrote a good deal of Russian verse at Cambridge, has on more than one occasion pointed out.

My poems are faces to me. They are persons, with peeves. They haven't, don't, come in Indian file, the way Chazal says egotism encounters feelings. They represent passions and positions. If you agree with them, I'm pleased. If not, be grateful you're more sensitive and intelligent than I. Some were easy to write, some difficult, others even born of a certain *angoisse*. Let me add that there are many poems not to be found here, some from my vernating stage, others from college when, overworked, I wrote many of a bumbling grumbling sort into lined notebooks which I later threw away. There is no single provenance to what I now see is a vast array of subjects and styles. I wrote "Lost in America" waiting in the Albuquerque airport. One or two I wrote in Leningrad. Some in England. Others in Mexico. Most of them at home on Cape Cod. I composed "The Hollywood Rag" in my head one morning walking down Santa Monica Boulevard in the sunshine. I believe I dreamt "Bridalveil Falls." Many of them I wrote years ago, some recently, most over the course of the intervening years.

Why did I turn to poetry? Ideas of a certain kind, thoughts of a certain nap, can properly be expressed in no other way, not merely one-take ideas, rather substances requiring a specific form, the way brandy suitably calls for a snifter, absinthe a drip glass, and champagne an eight-ounce "tulip." Any vehicle of a creative sort is a challenge, furthermore, and to discover a way to say things or to paint things or to sing things is arguably to have them already half done. A better question, I suppose, is why write at all, but to be a writer and to avoid writing is worse than an internment, it's to be interred. "There is no life except in the word of it," wrote Wallace Stevens, who in saying so only recapitulated solid theology. And when did I write these poems? Snatched time, for the most part. Does anyone do such things full-time? Of course, where more deliberation would have improved many of them, over-reflectiveness may well have drained the initial fervor. I find the intensity of working on a poem like first love, a heady drug. And isn't opium to the Chinese an extra form of daylight? Whatever interrupts your work is invariably unimportant. I hate telephones and on my way to the post office almost always say a prayer that my mailbox is empty. But it's true, we're all of us being badgered half the time for no good reason. (I've always thought it revealing that the Visitor from Porlock was an insurance salesman.) I loathe writers' colonies, groups, conferences. I am not a Romantic nor a mystic scorning life. I have vision but few illusions. I am not afraid to trust the imagination. I am curious, like most writers, about many things and write poetry the way I live, entering all traps, as Kazantzakis once put it, like some extremely elastic rat, which enters the trap, eats the mixture set to catch it, and then simply goes on to other traps, well aware that the last trap, the trap of Death, awaits us all.

It has been suggested that modern poetry is frequently derivative in manner from the conversation poems of Coleridge. The many voices of Browning. And Hopkins, with his directness, his love of words, his colloquialisms of rhythm and language. And of course Swinburne, the "Red Dwarf of Balliol." I have many favorites. Shakespeare, of course. Milton, especially. The Jacobeans. Middleton. Tourneur. John Webster. Pope. Swift. Keats. Dickinson. Yeats. Wallace Stevens, Philip Larkin. I was in touch with poetry even as a youngster, when rhythm had a great effect on me. I can hearken back to those enchanted nights when my parents, taking turns, read to us by candlelight "The Wreck of the Hesperus" and "Barbara Frietchie" and "Annabel Lee." I depended on sound as much as on sense for what seemed crucially necessary for poetic flight. In storybooks. Weekly readers. Even prayers. Ancient intonations from the liturgy of the Church like the rolling "Suscipiat" or phrases like *incedo dum affligit me inimicus,* or hymns like "Regina Coeli" and "Pange Lingua" which I repeatedly heard as an altar boy.

Wordsworth is of course correct in his suggested assertion that as children we're in touch with ideals and immortal ideas. I would sing with delight even as a boy as words in all colors and keys came to me simply by being alive. I *thought* poems, unselfconsciously drew them all over my papers. Most of my favorite early books were poetry, with big print and splendid illustrations. The dream life I sustained was the most important part of my childhood, and certainly the best of it. I was alert to words as play in an arbitrary game whose criteria of pattern and symmetry led to elusive visions that made me mad with admiration.

Dreaming, like writing, is a solitary act. There are visions that can be realized only by coming to terms with them yourself. I've always had the feeling I should experience things alone. That way, I felt, they would count. I recall some apposite lines from *Eugene Onegin:*

> . . . all poets
> are friends of fancifying love.
> It used to happen that dear objects
> I'd dream of, and my soul
> preserved their secret image;
> the Muse revived them later.

Poetry, like any art, takes place on those particular occasions that need more than facts. A universe is circumscribed, an epistemology involved, but poetry deals not merely with veracity. A real artist never gives himself over to visual quotation. Opinions are not retinal. A paradox emerges. In a very real sense, the closer you approximate what you see, the more you tend to betray the art of the regarding you. There should be as much of the painter in a portrait as of his sitter. We write to get a second chance in life, in the way of young Prince Hal, to "redeem the time." In "Notes Toward a Supreme Fiction," Wallace Stevens ascribes the making of art to our *foreignness* in the world, and to our desire for a compensatory native world. He writes, "From this the poem"—it could be any art—"springs: that we live in a place / That is not our own and, much more, not ourselves." Surely artists are, have always been, the first to see and to know and to feel the asperity of all that. "To know the world, one must construct it," wrote Cesare Pavese. And of course he's correct.

I take poetry seriously. I wrote none of these poems merely as a diversion. Writing anything as a dabbler has not so much never interested me as never occurred to me. Talent goes in several directions anyway. Most people perhaps fail to realize this. It has always amused me the way small, cheeseparing, turf-defending academic apparatchiks, ignoring Poe, James, Yeats, Proust, Eliot, et al., contemptuously look down on novelists and poets as critics, invidiously finding themselves at enmity with the very artists they're so desperately trying to emulate and, ludicrously, even supplant. Deconstruction, after all, is not only self-congratulatory but more often than not the moon-desperate attempt on the part of literary critics with all their bilge and bile and obfuscation to claim that they themselves are also creative. ("Melville of course didn't realize it himself, but what he was trying to say in *Moby-Dick* was . . .") No wonder Gautier called critics eunuchs.

I put this volume together over a period when I was not teaching, a duration of some length when I had more time than usual to do so. Thereby hangs a tale. It began with my being involved in an imbroglio at Yale in 1988 for having had the audacity to call six rapists "monkeys"—I was using the word in the sense of "*moitié singes,*" as Voltaire satirically described the French—who in a savage and sub-human way had set upon a jogger in Central Park, mercilessly beat her, two of them holding her down while the other four raped her. And then they left her to die. Eighty percent of her blood had been spilled. A black child psychologist from Harvard named Alvin Poussaint within the week went on a television talk show and said the rapists, who were also black, were "angry" (his word), implying, at least to me, not only that their actions involved a sort of social protest but that they were somehow relatively blameless or misunderstood. Even years later, after two fatal shootings at Thomas Jefferson High School in Brooklyn, Poussaint again appeared on the *Today Show* (Feb. 28, 1992) and blamed the trouble on handguns, like a cook blaming his spatula for burning a sheet of cookies, and not only referred to the killers as "children" but described them as "frustrated," a word normally ascribed to someone who loses a key or breaks a shoelace or has to wait in line.

Finding Poussaint's tendentiousness worse than his stupidity, I immediately fired off a letter pointing out to him, using an injudicious word or two, I don't deny—as of course he himself had in his apologia for the rapists—that it was precisely his kind of indiscriminate defense that created racists in the white community. My letter to him, while angry, was clearly not racial. It didn't matter to Poussaint. He accused me of racism and questioned my worth as a professor, alerting various people at Yale from my frightened department head to certain students in the Afro-American Club to apparently anybody he knew in New Haven in an implicit if not explicit attempt to get me fired, creating a storm of controversy on campus in the process, including a spate of undergraduate articles, each one dumber than the next, in the yellow college journals there with which we're all familiar ("Hello, history? Get me rewrite!") and which I sought to rebut. There weren't the slightest grounds of course for such a course of action.

But I was not rehired, a subtler ploy, of course, and bloodless. From the deans on down to department heads to the faculty, Yale is, much of it, an effete nest of weak and charmless indefinites, sexless males and literary and political termagants, many of whom, educated beyond their intelligence, are more interested in doing what's safe or politically advantageous than what is right. Not one woman, faculty or student, stepped forward to say a word on my behalf. Nor apparently did it occur to any of them to read my novels, *Three Wogs* and

Darconville's Cat, which, among other things, are wholesale vilifications of prejudice, bigotry, and racism. But that involved reading, and this was a college, and who had the time? I was astonished at the general upsidedownedness in the whole matter. And the craven denial was appalling. What diplomacy in the world should allow a person to sit on his hands when someone is savaged as that poor woman had been in Central Park? Not even Du Cange's dictionary of low Latin contains that definition.

As a final around-the-end move, Poussaint passed on the letter I wrote to him (unless of course, by some pure coincidence or other, the reporter in question here was an inveterate reader of the *Yale Daily*) to an irresponsible hack at the *Boston Globe* named Derrick Jackson, also black, who, quoting only half of my letter while creatively editing out the significant passage clearly proving me nonracist—with or without venal advice to do so I can't say—then proceeded to attack me in several semiliterate columns of choplogic for being one, ironically opening up these dopes in their chicane to the very charges they made against me.

In any case, exile, rustication, whatever you choose to call it, was a blessing. It allowed me not only time to write but confirmed in me a resolve—finally—never to teach again if I can avoid it. After twenty-two years of teaching, I was spared wasting any more time with academic hairdressers and literary accountants and faculty fakers. The heady air I breathed upon my release! The sudden freedom! It first hit me with a climax of incredulity, then I was footloose and away. Banishment, like a death sentence, can concentrate the mind wonderfully. And I was given a whole new lease on life. Henry Thoreau felt a similar buoyancy after his teaching stint failed. So did Dante, who was to be condemned to death, remember, if ever he set foot in Firenze again. He never returned to his native city but later enjoyed the symmetry of putting many of its citizens in hell. His own teacher, Brunetto Latini, told him:

> "That ungrateful and malignant people
> because of your good deeds will be your foe:
> small wonder, since among the bitter berries
> it is not right for the sweet fig to flourish."

Let me acknowledge, while on this negative note, that a good many of the poems included here are doom-dark, products, as it were, more of midnight than of noon. I make no apologies. There are many things that irk me to no end but about which in these poems I've not said a word, like nationalism (the cause of wars); Boston sports writers; the word *dude;* ham; games in which self-appreciation is intrinsic;

television; three-bean salad; American overfamiliarity; small-souled statisticians; evangelists; wasting food; gossipy talk show hosts who, feigning sympathy for their guests, actually exploit them; entertainers who change their names, surely among the worst lies on earth; doctors, and of course their thieving counterparts, lawyers; Rothko's paintings; the pastel colors of American cars; cement-paved children's playgrounds; minimalism; window-ledge cookery; all politicians (retroactive); people who use the expression "by and large"; foursome dinners; telephone callers who, failing to reach you, never consider writing a letter; and the current co-optation by a populist history-on-the-march that disregards politeness, grace, and the truth of the Gospels, dispositive proof not that the end of the world is imminent —I'm not that dramatic—but that the Goths are once again at the gates.

Orthodoxy is reticence, nevertheless, prudery a form of avarice. I've written my poems without coyness and made it a point of saying anything I wanted to of what I've felt. Many people nowadays seem to think that holding opinions is a form of bad manners. There was a time in this country, believe it or not, when having convictions and maintaining one's principles was not only expected of people but more or less determined a person's worth. Not any longer. It's not popular. We prefer conformity, self-consciousness, hypocrisy, and cowardice. Writing poetry is like going to confession: telling the truth is paramount. But haven't we been assured, by a believer in both, that all we need to know is that Truth is Beauty? The fact is, most actions, like a good many thoughts in the minds of a good many people—just like the people themselves—have a dark side, and truth is the only thing that makes you free.

For a while there I took the time to send certain of my poems out to various magazines. Often they came back within days, unbought and, for all I know, unread. Many editors can't tell a good poem from a proctoscope exam. There is also a lot of envy among poetry editors, and many secretly insist on pedigree and despise genre-jumping, like the fat, monstrous and melancholy pedant we have on a classical radio station in Boston, a disc jockey, mind you, who makes it a point never to give the Celtics scores in the morning simply because in his mind no one who likes Beethoven could possibly like basketball. I sent poems to the *New Yorker* and to the *Atlantic,* magazines that are run in a sort of gated-off or hermetic way like clubs or fraternities with closed membership and special codes. Whereas at first the rejections bothered me, they soon began to amuse me. It made me send editors only more of them, so they'd feel bad. I didn't care if they *did* feel bad. I only know that they should have. And so to me they did.

I have chosen to put these many poems in alphabetical rather than chronological order, since I never took the time to date them and couldn't possibly remember any significant sequence. "A poem is an absence," wrote Wallace Fowlie, "a poem is an effigy." Who was it pointed out that in the absence before poems begin, poems begin? All's over before a poem happens. And yet we write to clarify, to characterize, what we've already thought. Poetry, to a degree, gracefully evades what it's talking about, artfully rearranges thought. Acting is certainly involved. And so consequently is disguise. There are arabesques. There's a picaresque aspect to it, as well, a voyaging outside the self. Poetry is strangely anti-Odyssean, a running *away* from home to find your identity. It is enigma. Henry David Thoreau once wrote, "It is only by a miracle that poetry is written at all. It is not recoverable thought. No definition of poetry is adequate unless it be poetry itself. The most accurate analysis by the rarest wisdom is yet insufficient, and the poet will instantly prove it false by setting aside its requisitions. It is indeed all that we do not know."

A writer's life, devoted, ideally, to coming to terms with it, a matter I have always seen less as the point than as the strict, even moral requirement of it, might be seen as a sort of staircase of which poems are not merely steps, or even parts of steps, but simply nails or reinforcements or kickboards. There is so much more above, beside, and underneath a poem. An ontology is involved. There is always a poem not printed on paper, coincident with the secret disposition to respond to that which feeds it. It is what the poet has become through his own work and how he has developed, a quite separate thing. One often feels, oddly, a quietistic distance from one's work. The meanings of poetry differ from those of proposition. A created thing is formed according to principles quite other than those which govern the expression of an opinion or the construction of an argument. The focus therefore must be on the poem, not the poet, because, as an imagined whole, the poem, if it convinces, brings into activity a field of resources richer than can be mustered by deliberated conviction or didactic intent, which is why, as is frequently the case, writers aren't necessarily reliable guides to their own work.

Apologists for poetic theory will, I hope, as to matters of content, be patient with if not satisfied by my observations in the fistful of poems I wrote dealing with the genre, "Ars Poetica," "Fiction's Fun to Feign," "The Lollipop Trollops," "Padre Todopoderoso," and "The Way to Cedar Rapids." I'm convinced, finally, one could have a kind of party with many of the characters who for weal or woe appear in these pages, though frankly most of them would be people I wouldn't invite.

I come finally to the place where convention calls upon one to express gratitude to Mr. Advice, Prof. Sine Qua Non, various librarians, even the unswerving dedication, say, of people like one's first-grade teacher, in my case Miss Purcell, who with a kind of prescient wisdom back at the Washington School saw the special way I had with words as she flashed vocabulary cards in front of my sober little face. The extension of my own thanks is both more limited, and more conceptual, I'm afraid, for it was time more than anything else that allowed me the chance to see this work come to anything like its final if not finished form. I have no doubt it would be more in the order of things to tender thanks to the Architect of Time, but whether time was given to me or whether I stole it still remains mysteriously and ultimately unclear, as what doesn't. With that said, my remarks needn't be prolonged except perhaps for one final word. I think it sociologically diagnostic to note that the license plate on Dr. Seuss's automobile read "GRINCH."

West Barnstable, Mass.
March 1992

It is not my fault, I assure you, that things occurred in the order in which they did occur. I am not the regulator of this universe.
                    —Frederick Rolfe, *The Desire and Pursuit of the Whole*

Admissions

When we take her upstairs in the attic,
It's as much a crossing over
As a going up, erect, like Bozo clowns,
For children in the tide.
And the running after noon to call
Sweet hellos and coos to her
Is as much a lying down for us, renown
As much as children for a ride,
In joycarts, on a slide, or for a fall.
And all the thrashes, mysteries,
The Easter lurches we take unfrighted,
Must become a dancing in the dark
As well as moaning in the night
When our apple-chested ladies, benighted
With our ribbons and our cozy flesh,
Know so little of our attic,
Or its ladder lying down or set aright,
That they don't dare chance one remark.
No, it's all geography and promises;
I'm afraid, the happy dancing over pears,
The boo-hooing dance when ordered to our bed;
We stand erect, we lie, or duck around the bend.
But running up a ladder,
Like making love,
Is running toward the end.

Alexander Theroux

I fear my name
As fear my name I should,
For sybils say
(It's quite the same)
A strange and silent motion's
Also found in wood.
Alexander let's discount
The great I couldn't, the great he could.
My surname's but
An ur-name, shut
To all discerning eyes and good.
The hero buried deep within
Without is shrouded by
Clumps of consonants and vowels;
And it we can't espy.
The rue I fear.
The rut its smut
One easily detects.
A surface has its symbol
As a galley ship its decks.
The royal r-e-x,
One notes,
Is threatened by a hex.
A sybil's not frenetic
To find the static so kinetic;
The *truly* enigmatic
Is the syncategorematic,
A truth at once accessible and new.
Pronounce it *throw*, pronounce it *threw*,
Thorough, thorax, Thoreau,
Whatever thing emphatic—
But when you find a route
You find a rue. I fear my name
As fear my name I should;
For sybils also say
Effects must fear their cause.
And what mostly gives me pause,
Mostly fear and mostly stir,
Is not the rut, the rex, the rue.
It mostly is the her.

Amelia Earhart

I've always loved your smile,
Your eyes of grey, the bell-like
Cheekbones of your face,
Your tapered hands,
A symbol of your flying grace,
Your tousled hair, the soft full lips.
What model out of *Vogue* ever showed
Such elegant slim hips?
You were known as "The Girl in Brown
Who Walks Alone" in several
Of the high schools you attended.
You had your own principles.
You wouldn't carry a comb.
You were a dreamer,
Needed to be free;
I don't believe a love affair had ended.
No doubt you were alone for want of me.
(Can I not dream dreams as you,
Rue as a man what as a woman
They said you couldn't do?)
"I'm still unsold on marriage,"
You once wrote.
"I don't want *anything* all the time."
I would have understood.

I've memorized your habits
Like the name that in repeating,
But which you mocked, I love.
You hated hats (for which I'm glad),
Would not drink tea or coffee,
Disliked hairpins,
Had a penchant for cotton shirts.
Particularly short-sleeved ones
Colored plaid,
In which you looked too thin.
You loved your Lockheed Vega,
Red and bold as you were shy.
Your avoirdupois aloft was gasoline
In a sort of perpetual duel;
Going against the precept

Virtually constituted a sin.
"Six added pounds" (I know, I know)
"Offset a gallon of fuel."
Did always keeping windows closed
In the cars and planes you drove
Indicate anything of dread?
"I don't like to be mussed up,"
You once, I thought enigmatically,
Made it a point to be said.

When you worked at the Settlement
On Tyler Street in Boston,
Denison House I knew,
Why couldn't I have been alive to bring
Your lunch, buttermilk (your favorite)
And sandwiches just for you?
We would have found a bench.
I would have let you rest your head
On my knee, right there, to pass the time.
I could have read you poems,
Which defined as much as clouds
What in your too brief life you held sublime
In those mile-high worlds above
Waiting for you to explore.
Is it so vain of me to think
What you were looking for,
When in that plane you flew so high,
Was really love? Why then,
Let vanity go on to say,
If at the end it was your fate
When falling from the sky,
If it had to be
And I could not have caught you,
I wish it was for me.

Andover Spires

You stand, old school, bright upon a hill,
Distinguished by two centuries' long reach,
But what of fools now hired there to teach,
Indifferent to the students that they kill
By snobbery, sloth, political intrigue,
Drones who rarely read, are voted pay
Not by merit or degrees but length of stay,
Conspirators to only those in league?
Spires are declarations of intent,
No more signs of education than
The poles effected to support a tent
Can guarantee who'll gather there by plan.
No need, Sam Phillips, however, to repent.
A blackness even Eden overran.

Anecdote of Santa Fé

On the reservation
Oné and Noné make posole.
They love each other
And so will stay

Together in the way
That blue needs brown
And brown needs blue
In Santa Fé.

As blue needs brown
And brown needs blue
Oné is as much a part
Of Noné in that way,

But though they stay,
Together Oné and Noné
Are neither one
Nor none in Santa Fé.

Are the Skeletons of Fat Men Fat

How find joy enough to survive
Our daily pain? No black-hat chef awaits
With tricks to pamper us with anything

Other than with refuse meats,
And that is Mr. Death with his umbrella
Unfurled above our every hope,

Frayed, sieved with holes,
A mockery of the bluer, higher vault
We wish of heaven's dome.

What awaits at the end of all things
Awaits by definition at the end of each,
So how then do we all imbibe our joy,

This fragile self with but
Fat enough for seven cakes of soap,
A spoonful of sulphur,

Iron equal to a one-inch nail,
Lime enough to whitewash a small shed,
An ounce of various metals,

Phosphorous for 2,200 matches,
Carbon equivalent of a 28-pound bag
Of musty unimpressive coke?

There is no cool capillary action
In the spirit. A skin forms, for instance,
Where moving water meets the air.

Surface tension. There is always
Someone in front, someone always behind.
But there, *that* is why

No heart is a Marianas Trench.
Just enough of hope resides to prevent
The weak neap tides of the heart

In knowing happily that next to us
Are only more fleshbags, whitewash, coke,
More fat for soap, sulphur spoonfuls,

Iron nails, more funny phosphorus
For the many kinds of flames in front and,
To tell the truth, more pink behinds.

Ars Poetica

What polishes, like gold
Transformed by art from moron metal,
Is what alone will shine.

Don't wise old cooks suspect
The way fluidity is always flux?
The liquid that they pour

Into their snouted spoons,
Exenterated by an artist of a kind,
Is not as wonderful?

Making's not what's being done
But rather finished. What we contain
In an array, to make perpetual

And true as a solid form of grace,
Must first have gone from potency
To act, a process of arrangement

No doubt Aunt Susanna Seacat
With her fabricopediac fingers
May call art. But is it?

The stuff of lace and lancets
Carted out to while away an afternoon?
Becoming isn't Being any more

Than what necessarily we're large
Enough to finish in those complications
Giving substance form. Oh Cellini,

Battilòro of coin and shield
And buckle! Your beauteous pizzopizza
Make me cry! Poems are tribute,

Each one a sacrament, a caelum,
Hosts in monstrances like mandala,
Rose windows all ablaze.

There's nothing wrong at first
With faking what you fist in clay.
Forge what isn't forged. But

Stay close to the scheme of God,
Otherwise what's fashioned isn't made.
Poems are hammered and distinct,

Of what once of course was molten
Precious and fluid and sweetly gold
As sesame oil in Szechwan.

Assumption

Found nowhere in the Bible
Is a single verse to justify
Mary being crowned in heaven.
Should we assume it's a lie?
Why do priests so fabricate?
To compensate by drama what
their own lives lack in scene?
Not to care what's corrupt?
Why not simply say she lived
in a house somewhat content
after a complicated public life
like any aging beauty queen,
praying, fasting, remembering
before she died a natural death
she gave birth at age fifteen
to a dark-eyed boy with a destiny,
survived for a quarter century
his death at thirty-three,
then sat outside the door?
Why any different from any mom
who understandably missed the son
she couldn't make gnocchi for?

Auden's Face

It was cracked like a Weetabix.
A pound, like ours, of funny dough
Thumbed to a play-face, nostrils to wicks,
The widish ears, appended last, for show.
Then was it cooked. A simple noun
Animated by the heat of verbs
Which best describe it, make it renown:
Runneled, tunneled, words that disturb.
Some say, old dackel, that all those frets—
An apple creased, a steppeland parched—
Were scored by the smoke of smoking cigarettes.
Your biscuit cheeks, so antique, starched,
Are those smirks? Frowns? A worry each line?
How with such wrinkles shows something so fine?

A un romancier de ma connaisance qui ne mesure qu' 1m 70

A la saison des Nobels, au printemps,
  Pour la gloire, le prestige et l'argent,
Naitront pléthore de voix,
  Mille sentiments de choix,
Des hourrahs meurtrissant les gorges qu'on deploie
  Il en sera le seul parent.

To a Novelist I Know
Who's Only 5'8"

At Nobel time in spring
  For glory, fame, and pelf,
Will come a plethora of votes,
  Sentiments of a thousand notes,
Cheers as if from aching throats,
  But only from himself.

Billy the Kid Questions the Dark

Young Henry McCarty roamed the Lower East Side
Stabbing boys and thieving coats from Chinamen
Virtually every week.

Don't killers stand before us all like questions
Calling to the jackal deep in the darkness
Of our own hearts to speak?

He beheaded cats with a broken pocketknife.
That someone could do such a thing to another
Involves us all in a way.

He developed a skill at monte and changed his name
Soon after murdering something like nineteen men
And settled in Santa Fé.

Who can't confess given this fallen world
That we all share in the desperate crimes of others
When darkness is all we know?

Where the healthy tear the sick apart
Nothing hale applies, and one
Remains another's foe.

One day he went to Fort Sumner to visit a girl,
Called out "*Quién es?*" in the darkness there.
Nothing more was said.

What does anyone find who questions the dark?
Anubis wearing pointed sheriff's ears
Tearing away your head.

Black Racist

What head isn't filled with feathers
That's black because it isn't white?
Yours, you say? Don't make me laugh!
Rhetoric is monkeyshines, like
Anything else. As if ventriloquists
Don't mutter like their cats!
You talk to me about compassion
Without showing some to me.
It's a fact that bigotry has paper walls.
You naughty nitwits with funny hats,
Public forums, and wagging cravats,
Who spoon tar with the best
Are no different than nobodaddy,
Including you with all your ballyhoo.
Dummies, for all their wood,
Fare like all the rest
Who cack bitter names in the night
And nothing on earth can make them
Seem less real or right
Sitting on their owner's shelves
Than words that they expect from you
That they love to cockadoodledoo
That they use to constantly boo-hoo
But never use themselves.

Blackwind at Prayer

Blackwind kneels in silence all alone.
He paints with yucca tips on skeletons of cows.
Bones are real. To him those bones are real,

Like boulders that inside us as we kneel
Measure our mortality, not might. But art endows
With blessings men who color bone,

Who dare approach a surface hard as stone
And leave on doleful dryness what the wind allows
To whiten after giving sol its meal.

Boogie Man Blues

For Clarence "Frogman" Henry

I'm a nightstick man, gone canoninize yo bitch.
I got a cat's black fever, enough to make you itch.
I scairt you born at the crossroads, caint you tell?
You howl night and day like my dog named Idabel.

We live in the Nickel thowt no coat and hat,
Used to greens n possum skilletfried wifout no fat;
Don't make no matter, I takes what comes to hand.
When you strut by I plunk yo elastic band.

I'm a watchwitch, lowdown, bluegum chocolate boy.
When I bop yo booty you gone ring-a-ding-ding with joy;
I barefoot with love which fill my guitar-case heart.
Yo can dig my mojo rising in the cotton cart.

I gone saltfish yo heart, come down like summer rain.
I gone disclose existence, cayenne pepper yo brain.
I gone dicker, dodder, doodle, n dodge yo jelly roll.
I got kisses like a screet-owl's sweet momma got soul.

I got the two-stage warble, got me a lion's mane.
I got a goosefoot root like to drive the mommas insane.
I gone plink, plank, plunk-a-doo-doo like a mumbo man,
I can cling, clang, clunk-achoo-choo jiggity jan.

I got sly boots for the askin, baby, turn it up.
I gone be bustin thoo yo walls to walk yo pup.
I make yo seedpods scatter, make you think.
We shake midnight, Momma, kettle and sink.

I got the magic motion in my poontanging fingers fo fun.
Get you loney dogs for lunchtime, RC Colas and rum.
When you hot pot dog trot, baby, I wan mess with you.
You be wantin to start bout when we gettin through.

Boston Irish Pols

You were not brought up on A Street
As much as spawned, ignorant as a dawn
Only the insincere get up to greet.
When you swept the wards by cadging votes
From lackeys with your coal-scuttle hands,
Who was shocked you wiped them on your coat?

You hate each other like the running pox,
Urban bog rats, unprincipled pimps of graft,
Greener in your envy than your shamrocks
When another of your kind succeeds.
"I knew him when he was *nothing*," comes the sneer,
To best assure (according to your creed)

No one, saving you, be seen as God.
You've been on the take for donkey's years,
Pulling strings for phonies, fakes, and frauds,
Feeding like a pink pig in a sty,
Burrowing in dirt beneath the State House
Searching out another dug for sucking dry.

Gifts, free tickets, bribes to pass a bill,
A pension huge, a car at state expense,
A parking space for you on Beacon Hill,
You jig and amble on Saint Patrick's Day
And play the stage buffoon to guarantee
The dopes supporting you remain that way.

Sexless faces, empty speeches, lies,
A narrow mind as thick as two short planks,
The Irish pol in Boston only tries
To fill his pockets. Therefore understand
His perfect description as an arse upon
Which everyone has sat except a man.

A Boston Marriage

Miss Amy Lowell was butch,
Miss Ada Russell was femme;
Lowell was mostly apple,
Russell was basically stem.

The former loved smoking cigars,
Chewing them down to the root;
The latter loved shopping on Tremont
In a perfectly tailored suit.

Amy was big-bummed and hefty
As she wrote her Imagist poems.
She ignored society's dictates
To attend to her chromosomes.

She referred to Ada as "Peter,"
Kept a favorite mustache cup.
Given to sleeping all day,
She many a night stayed up.

When Amy and Ada went walking
On Beacon Street now and again
The couple quite symmetrically
Resembled a number 10.

"Her work's not creative," said critics,
"Only reproductive," they said—
An irony not lost on two women
Who explored each other in bed.

They intentionally flouted convention,
Traveled the whole world round;
They had friends all over Europe,
Aldington, Lawrence, and Pound.

The man who wrote *Lady Chatterley*
One night peeked into their rooms
And saw, through a haze of cheroot smoke,
They slept in the fashion of spoons.

H. D. once gave them a gift
Of some lavender beeswax candles,
Which in turn Amy gave to Ada
While Ada held Amy's "love handles."

That masquerade ball in Venice?
Strong roles must balance the weak.
"I'm Queen Christina," said Amy.
Whispered Ada, "I'll be a leek."

They usually got along well,
Their spats uncommon and few.
"*Turning?*" asked Ada, indignant,
One time in a Trinity pew,

When Ada, holding a hymnbook,
And this before dinner at eight,
Moved to give berth in a gesture
As if criticizing her weight.

"You are no better than Sappho
Or Joan of Arc!" Amy snapped,
Stressing their martial behavior
(The allusions were hurtfully apt).

What can you expect of a woman
Whose lifetime was given to verse?
Ada Russell, coolly indignant,
Replied, "At least I'm not worse."

What could be truer in Boston,
The home of the bean and the cod?
Nobody's anything, trust me,
If they're not particularly odd.

It would *never* matter to Amy,
And the same goes for Ada, as well,
Which of the two had the ding-dong,
Which of the two had the bell.

Brahms

Do the high violins of your Symphony no. 1
   In C Minor, op. 68
Confess the loneliness in what I hear,
   Not of wails or tears,
But of inner loss and sorrow?
   The calling horns like voices
Announce mysteries, distances, things
   That make me tremble.
Are you telling us, like James's Strether
   Or Wittgenstein in Norway lonely
With his mind, to *live?*
   Does being alone at least provide
An inner life with which to cope?
   To hope, when maybe something isn't there,
Or isn't there to learn?
   The future, becoming past so fast,
Leaves us only where we were
   To suffer loss, to burn.
It takes strength to live alone,
   And is often more than I can bear.
If that courageous music in the face
   Of what you know and I suspect
Must so increase our pain,
   As beauty often calls up loss
As if it were its share,
   Rescue us at least from what,
When we're alone, like you,
   We have to learn to gain.

Bridalveil Falls

For Caroline Langston

I'd never seen you,
Missed nothing I never had,
But the day that you came by
I died in my heart for beauty
As we caught each other's eye.

The following morn
I woke in the wild of my bed,
Impaled by the moon's white beams.
Had you come to my soul in a vision?
Had I met you there only in dreams?

I roamed the hills
For endless months with words
That formed in my heart like pain.
It seemed I traveled forever,
Though you never once came again.

If you exist
I wonder since you have gone
And I'm left to stare at the wall,
If I should curse or bless
The fact that I'd seen you at all.

By the Waters Now of Doom I Sit

By the waters now of doom I sit
Feeling with the sand my fingers,
Historical and long.
There's no memory forgotten,
I'll be sure, from Egypt when
The aching Jews with dripping clouts
Flitted through the night:
The Adam's people's yellings to be free,
Psalted,
Infected,
Null and void,
Just too damn tired of hammering
With nutlike fists
The granaries of tin.
Pharaoh unsuspected them, clammering,
And glugged his shandies off his wrist
Amid his women's cordial groans,
When—zap!—like dough shells
All the Gypsies bleated in their shower caps
And died.
Things that happen fast are
Very often meaningful, and linger;
By the waters now of doom I sit
Feeling with the sand my fingers,
Historical and long.

Café du Télégraphe Anglais

What cook who makes a poisoned pie
Will agree, by what he does, he doesn't dream?
I told you, mediocrity's a cinch.

The argument we had in Tangier
Made two reflections on the subject, not one,
But upset less than two people,

Our love was so confused by talk.
The very act of doing does away with thought,
Like Arabs being bilked by traders,

Their noses close to coins as scrolls,
Who ignore their pain to fumble up their gain.
But being in the desert dreaming of God

Is not eating dessert of spotted dog.
We need each other to contest what otherwise
Is killed by what's ignored.

I can even take your theater French,
Amy of America, to sad things unexplained
And left to die like that.

There are dracos in the darkness,
Arabs in burnooses who color the air they run,
Like shadows. Isn't talk however hope,

Even if it hurts? White tainted pies,
Like lies, by talk and thought can be examined,
Not so when being wolfed.

Deliberation brings illumination to the mind.
Forget the waiter. You know what's important? Knowing.
And even more. Knowing knowing's.

Camera Lucida

1

Bowls of snibbled beans,
A slave in muslin padding down
An alley wearing tchipships,

A kiss in the Joe Pyeweed,
Striped awnings, São Paolo in the rain,
Some Carpathian prince.

Every form correctly seen
Is beautiful, concluded Goethe,
Not a photographer

But a man who knew a poem
Contrived itself around a way of looking
Out of who and what you are.

Hard? It's only a camera,
Not the Gofriller gamba you pretend it is
Waiting for your touch,

Though you unshy shutterbugs
Make up quartets of pains-in-the-ass
Just by being yourselves.

Few people have the imagination
Of reality. Few dare imaginatively
To glimpse it as it is.

Any craptoad in Andover
With sheets of just-wet snapshots
Can make claims for art.

The camera is cold. The eunuch
Behind it if unable to impose meaning
Beyond that through which he peers

Adds no poetry to what he sees,
Only saves to sell for stupidity to see
Paper crammmed with gewgaws.

2

Ho, Nutrix, feed me.
No muse is a meddler, no intimacy
Ever really unearned.

Make me by myself be me,
So by the occasion of being what I am
Not be the gist of what I make

But making out of what I see
Transform reality by making me meet
What I alone can transform.

No ice can set you on fire
But yourself, as Turandot well knew,
Yourself with a singular soul,

Unlike the quack in Andover
With his sprockets, snoots, and strobes
Who fakes what he can't find.

Product is not the point.
It is not a question of making art, but
Of making art of what you do.

What Lithuania without bears,
However, can be made to have them roaring
Just by fancy dreams?

A mind that is too flexible
Is powerless to restrain, I've seen,
The dialects of its own moves,

Although for want of a bear's
We can substitute a boiling ocean's rage
For roaring in a cage.

When is there never a taste
Of nothingness itself in the roar
Of a crashing ocean?

Talent can be horrifying,
In the way a photograph becomes a secret
Of only yet another secret.

We are always more or less
Than what we create by vision or void.
We run like fright, for artists

In being set apart resemble slaves
In low dry deserts or princes up on mountains
Where few decide to pup their tents.

Imagination also makes us live,
We who would create, in states of heightened
Crises that disturb and kill,

As we bide time in darkrooms,
In attempts at finding comfort with solutions
Even if they can't be seen.

Everyone suffers from the limitation
Of being only one person, while art requests,
Suggests we be more than what we are,

Lest dreams become an odd defense
Against awareness in a certain kind of mind
And never help or heighten it.

Images are there for us to see,
For such as those who look beyond excuse
To see above their fat equipment.

Forget Andover and its pedant.
Thought, remember, is a motion that divides.
Look hard, for palmary subjects abound.

Wends. Sorbs. Slaves. In no matter
What Carpathia are counts and princes
Boasting to be real.

Cat Noises

Who makes a kind of crowing, clacks its teeth at birds
Like maracas, chiclets, blows notes in flatted thirds?
Cats! Night's the sax. Egypt with its cult of cat
Worshiped all those mutt-whines, owl-howls, bat-spats,
Creaking doors, sounds a guitarist plicks with a plack,
A bumming top's spin, the winding of a watch's stem.
I once even heard one moo. Hectoring is big with them.
Leave one for a day. *"Bite my bum!"* he'll quack.
Mine once lost in the woods became an electric drill.
A throaty wire-drawn-out whine like stretching twine
Which soon becomes low thunder accompanies a kill.
Yours, for example, which would frankly suit them fine.

Catharine

Your alias might have been
Miss Harriet Brown,
The serviceable shoes, peevish cats,
The way you ate,
Your jutting jaw,
Your glasses out of date.
Then math, your books,
Your hair too thick,
Too low a forehead for
Orthodox good looks.
No play of fancy ever lit your smile;
Your pinched-out emotions,
Graceless and tight,
Resembled for me the falling of night.
Your silly brother whose calendars
You feigned to love at Christmas
Just to keep him sane
Loved hockey, worshiped teams,
Bought tickets in the pouring rain.
The fool had a passion—
At least give him that.
You measured tit and gave only tat.
Surely no one like you becomes so cold
Without the benefit of a shaping mold.
What of your parents?
Queer father, promiscuous mom,
May I ask, was your divorce together,
Even half as bad
As what separately you've become?
Or was it what you caused
Over what you grieved?
A dope of a son,
So earnest and so bent;
A daughter who believed
The less she wrote
The more she felt
You didn't deserve the letters
That she never sent.

Chirico by Chirico

Original men must have wandered through a world full of
uncanny signs.
                    —Giorgio de Chirico, *Mystery and Creation* (1913)

The steeple clock marks half-past twelve.
The sun is high and burning in the sky.
It lights houses, palaces, and porticoes,

Their shadows on the ground describing squares,
Rectangles, trapezoids of so soft a black
The burned eye can refresh itself in them.

What light. How sweet to be able to live
Near consoling gates, porticoes, arcades of
Black and white. No color. But what light.

And the absence of storms, of crying owls,
Of seas. Here Homer would have found no songs.
A hearse has been waiting forever.

It is as black as hope, and waiting forever.
There is a room with shutters always closed.
Somewhere is a corpse one cannot see.

The colonnades are empty, black and white.
Shadows both console and fail to console
In the way they fall by the way we feel.

A want of life awaits in colonnades.
Everywhere the sun rules. Shadows console
Sometimes. Precise geometric shadows

Of such starkness. One cannot count the lines.
Sadness. Nothing. The endless walls and arches.
The soul follows and tries to grow with them.

A garden gate is making you suffer
By premeditated geometries that run
The length of shadows right to left.

What in the way of refuge can we speak of
When we speak of porticoes and colonnades
That are empty, black and white?

Ancient lines, fitful lights and shadows.
The sun is setting. It is time to leave.
The clock marks twelve thirty-two.

A Christmas Pome

Christmas dinner had melon for dessert,
And he ate out the belly into the shell.
Tableau: Dad tuning for carols on the
   radio with his own kind of priestcraft;
Mom skipping with her trashy kettles
   into the silver air of night on the
   back porch.

Christmas day has its search for peace
   and epigrams,
And well-fed paternalists explain with
   cheeps and ovine grins the God
   who rusts iron and ripens corn and
Dismantles heaven for the dumbos.

Christmastime will have its troubles,
But not for college girls, the ones
   who want Just One Good Goofy Time,
   or paid comedians;
I mean bummies who had the horror of
   being duped, beyond the pale
   in their greasy bush jackets.

Christmas week has its messages,
Some are breathless hugs, a kissing
   with the hips in the upper room,
Or aunts whispering low to servants
   to be sure to braise the hen
   for Charles the Fat.

Christmas as a yule has its preparations,
Some against the scary snap that happens
   underneath the children's tent,
The slipping of foundations in the granddad,
   who refuses his sugar at the bottom of
   the lemonade, and
Pisses on his sheets in an upper room.

Christmas has its promise of bigness,
When kiddos, heavy with their polished teeth,
    scrunch into their dolls
With glossy foreheads, beyond the pale,
    and dance in the pattern of moonlight;
    remembering the butter reflected in
    their brothers' rims,
They climb in their joycarts and move on.

Christmas, finally, has its universe of dwarfs,
    monks, and warmen; those real morons
Who, sure as history, rap their stubs together
In grotesque applause at mysteries they
    haven't solved,
And ask their sweethearts, Haven't I been sweet?
I say sweetness, like Christmas, and leeks,
    is best when boiled.

"Circle" Burke

"Circle" Burke was a nasty piece of work
And smelled. Even as a boy he weighed
Over two hundred fifty lubberly pounds and was fatter
Than the food he fed on, wolfing doughnuts,
Ring-Dings by the fistful. And Moon Pies.
At fifty-two, he lived alone. He was Irish,
Never married. When he got depressed, he'd
Crawl up into a ball and hum show tunes.
He was impotent. He found dead gods.
He ate everything, pizza especially.
At midnight he often went for slices
By himself, sweating in his undershorts,
Soiled, heading down to the bar.

I was reminded of him recently,
Reading somewhere that the oldest letter
In our alphabet is in fact the letter O,
That prodromic nightmare, certain oaf,
Having held its round unchanging shape
Since the Phoenicians formed it in 1300 B.C.
Isn't character destiny? Fate what we are?
One night I slept with his ex-girlfriend.
Whereupon he creepycrawled her house
And punctured two front tires in spite,
Coming to despise what first he hated
Strictly because of what he saw he was.
Round things he hated. And fat.

Cocaine Cat

Shoot it, baby,
You can taste
A doctor's office
In back of yo throat,
Was all I said.
I handed her the set of toys,
Syringe, needle, and tie,
And say Merry Cripmas.
She hot for boy, do you
Understand was all?
Get me some cold fruit juice,
Motherfucker, she say out the open window
To no one, and grind her teeth.
I took a hit myself
And put away the toys.
Things stiffened.
She feel funky? Good.
I slamdunked her
Wif my lovemonkey.
She cried, see
What I'm sayin?
Then the bitch
Died, like
Jumped.

Cochiti Love

Gravures are kisses.
And then those hoops.
Cochiti make patterns
That go in loops.

Love's not straight.
Court with an eye
For pueblo designs
On pots that dry.

Colloquy with Miss Rita Hayworth

When you touch me, there is silver up my back,
a dance down Hollywood Road, Chinese nights,
racehorses poised like shotguns behind hot gates,
ready to break. There is no questioning it, manductress.
It is skylight, measurelessness in my mitts,
a gaze for the grace that is unaware of itself.
Won't you count the ducats piling in my heart,
swap gold, only for your fingers there to tease,
twiddle values out of me like coin, that you might
buy me cheap, naked as night, your slave?

Communion Tongues

Were you ever an altar boy
And had to pass the plate?
(The phrase is '50s Catholic
And probably out-of-date.)

Each and every communicant
Knelt there stiff as a post
Sticking out his or her tongue
To receive the wafer, or Host.

Such an array of tongues
A monster movie could claim,
Most of them frankly disgusting,
No two of them quite the same.

Sizes, all colors, and shapes
Ran the entire spectrum.
Some huge and puffy and swollen,
Others small as a plectrum.

Coins, checkers, phalloi,
U- and V-shaped and wet,
One or two loomed like a helmet's
Plume on a fat majorette.

Some fairly resembled slugs,
Bulbous and smooth and pink,
Others were fissured and grooved
And white as a porcelain sink.

Look at that wagging white one.
Is it a tongue or a beak?
Half a ruined Napoleon?
A piece of cracknel antique?

Stocky men had blunt ones.
Spinsters' tended to fork,
Children's were round and rosy,
Fat men had loins of pork.

Sickly kids displayed
Tongues red as a new Toyota,
Old folks broken moonscapes
Like the badlands of Dakota.

Pretty girls showed seedcakes.
One boy flicked his like a lizard
Which, stained from a purple gumball,
Gave it the hue of a gizzard.

Far too many were icky,
Membraneous and coated with yuck;
Some hadn't a trace of moisture,
Dry as a corn in its shuck.

A certain tongue seemed chamfered
On the tall and angular sort
Whose cross-hatching patterns recalled
The mazes at Hampton Court.

Many seemed bisected by
A parapsidal furrow,
An uncanny sort of trail
Recalling a gerbil's burrow.

Betting chips I saw,
Complete with fissured edges.
Two poked out like cheeses
Triangularly cut in wedges.

A lot looked just like coasters
While others not so flat
Revealed the wimbling tip
Of a hideous vampire bat.

Pointed ones seemed evil,
Sharper than winery bungs.
Another horror included
Senior citizen tongues,

Dry and rumpled and green
Like the floor of a witch's hovel.
And what about those protrusions
Long as a biscuit shovel?

Want to hear a confession,
Kind of climax to a play,
Of how I was even affected
In a personal sort of way?

Years later at the drive-in
When I was a teenage boy,
Though I was never a prude,
I suffered delimited joy.

My urges were healthy and normal.
I promise, I wasn't remiss,
Except for this single stricture:
I would never French-kiss.

Contrasting Fruitage

Would the girl I took to see
South Pacific in 1957, if she reads this,
Please try to contact me?

One rainy Saturday night,
We took my parents' old maroon Dodge.
I had two tickets in the loge.

You had on wicked silver shorts,
Were shy, wore a gardenia in your hair,
Whose scent went down inside me

Like a long white string.
Sitting beside your beauty in the dark
Gave me warm reflections

As full of technicolor as the Jujyfruits
I was too embarrassed to pronounce to buy,
And when you went to the ladies' room

I wolfed the tub of popcorn that made
My cheeks far slicker than my oily hair.
You bought a box of Nonpareils,

Which you delicately pointed to
In silence and had the grace to eat them,
One by one, with finger and thumb,

When in the dark our glances met
Just as Liat and Lieutenant Cable kissed.
And so we did the same.

Your lips tasted warm as cocoa,
A tropical heat in the bold blush I felt,
Leaving me a joyous deafness

I ascribed to thrumming theater speakers
When those lusty sailors burst out in choral song.
How unlike the morts I met in later life,

Crude Camilles and Creepy Cathys,
With shapes like pears, fists like powercats,
No conversation, and big hair,

Their tits deader than bagpipes,
Never mangoes, not those swollen flowers,
Rose and white and heather,

Which in the Polynesia of that Paramount
My buttery fingers tentatively unfurled to pat,
When magic gave to mystery

What more informs my memory
Than any lovely place named Bali-Hai.
And I can't remember your name.

Counterparts

Spare me the girl whose best friend is her mother.
Ready with the word to set her right;
Let a lad appear, and she can't find another
Reason for disliking him on sight.

I knew a woman in New Jersey once
Whose husband was a burden on her soul.
After their divorce this banking dunce
Left his bitter partner in a hole.

By this I don't mean money was the thing
That came between the woman and her kids;
It was the low suspicions that she'd bring
To every small activity they did.

She had affairs with half the men she knew
At work, in school (she took a course at night);
So how could she avoid from staining blue
Any subject that initially was white?

The evil here, implicit, is the blame
Passed on as if by magic to the daughter
That in each circumstance she'd do the same.
And any man involved? No less a rotter.

Jilted, jaded, homely, out of sorts,
This woman's life became what she conveyed;
No daughter, when faced with such reports,
Conceives of anything but innocence betrayed.

The danger in relationships like this
Is that the daughter then becomes the mate;
Responding otherwise would seem remiss,
And so becoming partners is their fate.

Thus like a married couple off they go,
For dinner, shopping, partners at the mall,
A week in Bermuda, to a Broadway show,
The daily expectation of a call.

No wonder then that love as it's defined
Can never penetrate the daughter's heart;
She deeply hates her father in her mind;
With her lamprey of a mother she can't part.

There are many who another's freedom want,
And many of those content to pass it on;
A ghost prefers an empty house to haunt,
But both are equally forlorn.

So having lived, mother knows what's best,
Advises daughter just what not to do,
And what does daughter think to pass the test:
Why, Mom, become a cripple just like you!

Creeping Judas

A very thin premeditated ghost,
He seems more predator when acting host
Than some hyena blinking in his lair
Who's at your side before you feel him there.
A hand like fog he slides around your waist,
With fingers cold that touch as if to taste.
Many roles he plays, like traveler wide,
Political pundit, companion at your side,
Critic, confessor, even acting dumb.
He's best by far at buttering your thumb.
A stiff uncanny stand-off air belies
The pink ambition in his shifting eyes.
He wets his finger and holds it to the air
To ascertain the proper face to wear.
A questioning informs his walking pace,
As he glides without a shadow, not a trace.
Scheming like Polonius he leads
Messengers to do his dirty deeds.
He subtly seeks to keep his reputation
Simon-pure from every connotation
Of public censure or any public wrong,
Needing to be lord of every throng.
He visits gardens, funerals to boot,
Goes to concerts, sports a tailored suit,
Flatters widows with his nasal bleat,
Smiles at every herbert on the street.
On Arbor Day he yearns to plant a tree
In a public square for everyone to see
His motives high. He also tends to go
On Sundays to a Negro church for show.
He'll mock a friend to titillate your taste,
Then snicker at the victim he's disgraced
Behind his back. He couldn't care a jot.
Once begin to care, you care a lot.
Snatching any pious chance to preach,
He's keen as spit to open up a breach
Between you and anyone he has the chance
To lure into his arachnoidal dance.
Your virtues he will praise aloud to friends
Yet lest a hand of friendship they extend

In your direction as he puffs you, be advised,
Drops darker hints of you to be surmised.
Success, you see, is not enough for him;
Others have to fail, remaining grim.
He'll say for your advancement he is keen,
So takes your side, pretends to intervene
In arguments where you've a lot to lose
And then by cunning twists of logic choose
To say the reverse of what will do you good,
Blurting out your faults in your defense
In mock attempts at trying to make sense.
If your suspicion leads you to complain,
Then his reply becomes the queer refrain,
"Why, doing just the opposite, old blue,
Is a form of imitation, too!"
Martial never flattered more than he
Or worked so hard in public to agree
With any fool who could advance his schemes,
Be the method craven or the means.
A friend to all who knows no loyalty,
He becomes for each just what they want to see.
Conformity becomes him like a drape
Which he wears satanically to ape
The kind of simple guilelessness he seeks
To murder by the havoc that he wreaks.
Truth and honor? Oh, for heaven's sake,
What's virtue when appearance is at stake?
He'll loudly threaten to resign the club
Of drunken sods who tendered you a snub,
Then turn around and suddenly appear
On a club committee he later comes to chair!
The treachery beneath such evil ways
Can plague a person to his final days.
Suppose your luck should take a bitter turn,
For instance, and the penalty you earn,
Leaving you to mount the gallows bleak,
Is so extreme you're not to live a week.
The state sets out to find among the mob
A hangman suitable to do the job.
Who will be the person that they bring
Twitching with a hempen rope to swing
You like a bolo to your fatal end?

Can't you guess? Why, everybody's friend!
He's as he was and is and long will be,
Your comrade true for all eternity!
If proof you need to have that he's sincere,
A phrase, say, or a gesture of his care,
He'll smile at you, the rope behind his hips,
And hissing *"Hail, Rabboni,"* kiss your lips.

For Roy Campbell

Criminal Man

Whether it's murder, rape, or the S & L scandal, crime costs
about $300 billion a year . . . a national tragedy. Why is crime
essentially a male pursuit?

—June Stephenson, *Men Are Not Cost-Effective*

For all the violence men create
Women are surely involved in the way
They flirt with whomever they mate
Like flash in electrical wire.
What more can one go on to say?
If prison inmates are 90 percent male,
Were they not first webbed in schemes,
Related to eros or love as frail
As hopes are entangled in dreams?
The sexual act is give and take,
When glowing hot flesh lights up
In passionate charge and abrupt
To fashion a fire with flames
Racing madly like me through you
And consuming us both in a pyre
Where nothing at all remains.
Isn't it true that men simply do
While women prefer to make?

Crow

Black flags, black rags,
Waving out of the nesting woods
High above the crags,

Be ever watchful when
Flying too low over rainy roods
Of trees and fen.

Men in blinds await
With no other thought but to kill,
As though your fate,

Being left to us,
Should be determined by our will.
Disposed of thus,

You're living proof
That we can bravely bring down heaven,
Vulnerable roof,

Kill what we can't face,
Less to justify than leaven
Our theology of waste.

Darconville's Sonnet

Love, O what if in my dreaming wild
I could for you another world arrange
Not known before, by waking undefiled,
Daring out of common sleep adventure strange
And shape immortal joy of mortal pain?
Art resembles that, you know—the kind of dare
Nestorians of old acknowledged vain:
"No, what human is, godhead cannot share!"
But what if in this other world you grieve,
Undone by what in glory is too bright,
Remembering of humankind you leave
That which pleased you of earthly delight?
Out then on art! I'll sleep but to wake—
Never to dream if never for your sake.

A Daughter's Confession

It wasn't him
I hated
Or any of the boys
I dated
To whom
I said good-bye.
My head is haunted.
It was my father's death
I wanted
In Quinton, N.J.,
Where he
First took his breath.

It wasn't them
I disliked,
All the girls
I knew
To whom
I never wrote.
Wrong waters fished.
It was my mother's death
I wished.
In Salem, N.J.,
Where she
First took her breath.

Deliriants

Almost old as powdered white
I left Athens late at night,
Tired in my rumpled suit,
Wishing in my hands for love,
For love had just relinquished
My powdered cracking hand,
Doom-eager, white as goat cheese,
Late at night in Athens,
Mad and quiet in its winking lights.
Smells of stone and burning meat,
Age, terror, promise. A *sirtaki*
Echoed from the outer dark.
I had left my coal brown Opel
Parked in Italy. I was taken
For a bummish messiah in Patras,
In my shorts, black from sun,
With my raven beauty,
Her there swinging her sandals,
Me a malicious enough cartoon.
We kissed in hooded doorways
Until she had to say good-bye.
Nothing to recount for others.
No parliament of friends would ask,
Bank on that, they wouldn't.
Silence, nightwind, lights.
There were no longer crones in black
Or cypresses standing sentinel
As I went trainward to Italy
And toward my coal brown Opel
Under a mandala of a moon
As round and bright and far away
As the imprint on my mouth
Of burning Grecian kisses.

Departmental Secretaries at Yale

You were both death on a bun,
Two bitches with bums spinnaker-fat,
Your white bryony hands, dead creepers,
Killing whatever you entwined, your perfume
Cheap as the envelopes you dispensed
With more spitting rancor than Alecto.
Not for you to hand out stationery,
Pencils, light bulbs free. Your mouths
Were bigger than your twats and those
Acid green supply cabinets you defended
Like phylacteries from Philistines.
"Paper just doesn't grow on trees,"
You sniveled at five o'clock, rushing
With your hair like tortured midnight
Out to meet your wistful husbands
Standing there like damaged penguins
Waiting by their cars out front for you
In the gloom of a New Haven dusk.
"Can't you meet with your students
In the corridor?" you once snapped,
Denying me an office, penny stamps,
A telephone, shoving your face at me
Like the dark blue thumbtacks you
Slowly, parsimoniously counted out
As if diamonds from the Ritz.
You disliked each other with an intensity
That suggested you both recognized
Something of yourself in what you saw.
Too used to being mean to feel
The need to kill, you found
Quite happily that pettiness alone
Sufficed to get and keep you high
Like those cheap orchids
You pinned on your tits at Christmas
Which forced to it, believe me,
We chipped in grudgingly to buy.

Emily Dickinson's Bread

In quiet Amherst
You cooked many munchy meals
And were good at it, too.

At supper table
Your stern father ate no bread
Not baked by you.

You lowered gingerbread
Eccentrically down to urchins
From an upper view.

When you won 75 cents
At the Cattle Show in 1856
With the money you drew

Did you buy some bones
For large and grumpy Carlo when
Barking himself blue?

Everyone's Fat Friend Is First to Coo

Everyone's fat friend is first to coo
love through the trebles in its face
rising like a cock to crow its song;

it is the sidekick that rubs lusts,
bold and armored with its *tho* and *chan,*
ribbon-lipped to smooch the darkness

that it swabs, not as if it had a soul,
but as if it had a heart, for flesh
by law has no soul even fit for darkness

of a kind, or of that kind it rises
to spelunk like a fool with its fat funds.
Great thieves merely hang the little ones.

Tableau: a fat acrobat swings to thrust
its trick above the nets surrounding it,
dumbly to perform. And though I stand

on him and am so high, so far above him,
still I worry that he brings me down,
for just as I gather myself to love,

my fat friend phones from where all phalloi
hug, from fountains where all huggers love,
and he is first to coo.

Février

Pour Lawanda Still

La neige, c'est cette tige étrange que l'on coupe a l'été:
Elle a un goût de noire écriture fine sur une page blanche.
Ce texte des foulées qui gaufrent le vélin
Fleure le quart d'eau de puits, au juillet chaud.

L'hiver balaie des dunes brûlantes de sable stérile
Et me rôtit la face comme un chien au désert.
Blanche, froide, une cendre légère descend du ciel aveugle,
Atterrit sur mon gant, cri aigu, doux bruit mat.

Alors que le vent éveille ma chair d'un claquement,
Je plante mes bottes dans la saison blanche et noire.
Sachant qu'au moindre arrêt, je disparaîtrai dans le neige,
J'entraîne ce mois à l'abri du premier seuil venu, et je souffle.

February

For Lawanda Still

Snow is the strange stalk out in summer:
It tastes of a thin black script on a white page.
A text of tracks pressed into vellum,
Smelling like a cup of well water in the heat of July.

Winter blows hot dunes of barren sand
And roasts my face like a dog in a desert.
A cold white ash glides down from the blind sky
And lands on my glove with a peep or a soft thud.

As the wind awakens my flesh with a crack,
I plant my boots in the black and white season.
Knowing that if I stop I'll disappear in the snow,
I march the month into any doorway and puff.

Fiction's Fun to Feign

Fiction's fun to feign. It mutters up the sleeve.
Aren't we mostly critics, failing to admit in masks
What our faces must reveal, of what most we hate
And so critics of ourselves? But answer what we ask?
Beleaguered by foolish sons and begging in-laws,
Didn't Dickens simply wire up with all his taints
Flinty Scrooge in the fury of his being bilked
From the bitter bile of his personal complaints?
Snatching sibyl's leaves often skews the sight.
"Easter Parade" is a secular song; Berlin kept it so.
"White Christmas" has nothing to do with Bethlehem.
It has to do with winter, it has to do with snow.
Dr. Seuss's Grinch is only Mr. Geisel's Jew
Irked as much by Christmas as by Gentile greed.
All writing is confession, duplicity in session.
Our imagination's more than anything our creed.

Formal Theater

Your eyes please keep
Above the puppet Man
And weep

But spare the rod
The operator's wrist
Is God.

Francesca da Rimini

Does the poetry of women lie
In being conquered? In the *Inferno*
You're far too ready to comply,
Crying, "O animal grazioso e benigno."
The tone, the adjectives of crouch,
To me reflect the nature of your soul.
The sin of obligation you avouch.
If Paolo's body won yours whole,
Brought about the fatal kiss that doomed
You to the windy space of hell, know
At least a man's fair form consumed
Your heart before the cold below.
Passion today has lost its purity:
Women swap their bodies for security.

Fr. Mario

Fr. Mario used to visit our house.
His eyes were crossed like a shithouse mouse.
He put me down for his own scenario.
A wicked priest was Fr. Mario.

He was our uncle and jimmy-jawed,
Pugnacious, tiny, and deeply flawed.
He drank bottles of Moxie, case upon case,
And spoke to people an inch from their face.

His collar was white, his mind was dark.
He once on a stroll to Webster Park
Stopped in the street, pinching my arm,
And hissed, "You're doing your mother harm!"

I wet the bed which he wouldn't forgive.
He sucked cigarettes like a Broadway spiv.
He sent us on errands across the street
And gave lordly advice with a nasal bleat.

He pinched girls' bottoms, squeezed our hands,
Took thirds at dinner, gave brisk commands,
"Study Italian!" "Don't fork the bread!"
"Get an afternoon job!" "Try using your head!"

He knew all the perks of being a priest,
Took subscribers on tour to the Middle East,
Collected Hummels, finagled free roasts.
Meeting Franco was one of his boasts.

He bumsucked the rich, cadged tickets for shows,
Kept shelves of good whiskey, row upon row,
Got turkeys at Christmas, sometimes the trees,
And of course for Mass cards took standard fees.

From all that he told us he ran the Church.
People in Rome if you wanted to search
Knew him at once, he said, merely by name.
Was it for me to question that fame?

My weaknesses, anyway, got him quite vexed.
He constantly shamed me on the subject of sex.
"Sissy," cried Mario, wagging his knife,
"Get married, you? You'd pee on your wife!

"You think a woman will turn a blind eye
While you hang a wet mattress out a window to dry?"
My heart almost stopped, missing a beat.
"Sleep on a bed with a cold rubber sheet?"

His mockery more by far than his screams
Polluted my nights with nightmarish dreams.
The Church I soon saw, when I came awake,
Was as tricky and cruel as a ten-foot snake.

At family gatherings for the longest time
(I never go but know chapter and rhyme)
Thanks are made to the good God above
And someone is chosen to discourse on love.

The homily's Mario's, now pathetic and old,
And he offers up prayers like a hypocrite bold.
He'll die in a bed surrounded by candles.
His coffin will shine and have real brass handles.

But in hell when he's screaming, almost insane,
And he calls upon someone to lessen the pain,
Howling for help from the hole in his face,
My dream's to appear and administer grace.

It's a symmetry due him without any reserve,
A fate one can't say he doesn't deserve.
Let eternity balance time and degree.
Dante himself would be quick to agree.

I'll locate the priest in the midst of the fire,
Roasting like Dives in a scorching hot pyre.
Seeing me suddenly, what will he think?
There'll be no Moxie to give him to drink.

Why not do what he knows I'm good at, OK,
That which he knew me for day after day?
I'll prove myself useful, if somewhat uncouth,
Stand on his head, and say, "Open your mouth."

The Gesture of Vanni Fucci

As reasonable as muffins
But sinister for all,
Rather than beginning
One's begun, that's all,
I lay as flat as quiet
New as color in my nudity,
Then sick at heart and sad
Tucked asleep in pins,
Sketched in hair
And wet as snow in my lanugo.
Incepted, bleak, and charred
With holy salt,
I grew in size,
Became brown with the best of them,
And fought my private wars,
Enjoying for the nonce
The paper stars I won
For more than being me.
I wait for number three
To see if I'll be sane:
I began when the Second War began,
And left for Europe on Bloomsday
Carried by the plane.
But if all that's said is ever done,
I mean, inceptions—
If they're repeatedly deceptions,
I know enough of figs to give them one.

The Girl Who Makes You Cry Is Always Love

The girl who makes you cry is always love,
    As dear as laughter,
    Expensive as your heart,
When night becomes as close as she,
    Embraces sweet as hair is warm
    Around her neck prompt the tears
That make a cry and therefore love.

The cry that makes you love is dear,
    For after hurt the laughter isn't there
    Nor the girl reflected in the song you sing
But only mirrored in the light
    Of what by broken hearts
    Is consequently learned of care
Which makes you cry and therefore love.

The love that makes your laughter real
    Is a cry that's kissed upon the mouth,
    The girl you taste and love,
A warmth you've hurt as close as night
    Who's angry from the eyes,
    Expensive as her heart, as dear as tears,
And makes you cry a laughter and a love.

God

Even the greatest man has to live in his own century.

—Ortega

When I take God upstairs,
Flip the light on, and
Provide him with the towel
Of my suggestion
To wash from the bowl on the stand,
I step downstairs, and he feels great harm
Like all old men,
And, whimpering, he stops with his cane
Until I take his plastic arm.

The Good Old Song

Wahoo-wa, Wahoo-wa.
—University of Virginia fight song

Buried in a yell is something from the throat.
That's what makes an old man old
And makes the eyes the yellow moon-dials
On the freshly slaughtered stoat.
There's a sound in the winestain, a sound in the ash,
In the licking of the jampuffs,
On the ice blue thighs of the majorette
And the swinging of her purple sash.
But I mean those musicless notes which hang in the air,
The yell which approaches a howl.
You thought I meant the whispers you make
Walking with Edna down the Lawn
As you kiss her in the sunset on the jowl?
That's the eunuch jamming on his pants.
Don't be mistaken: he's gone for Mommy's taffetas
With his white hand wrapped around his dime;
Careless of philosophy, he's careless of his dance.
But these are noises old as time
And stoats are butchered with a difference lance.
Listen for a yell, it's not a squeal
Like girlies who love to hee-hee in the dark
And, heated like those desert plants,
Let their puffy hands provide exactly their appeal.
That's only the noise or the plastic arm
In the plastic overcoat.
Buried in a yell is something from the throat.
It's not, you see, Dick Whittington turning on his toe.
A yell you'd call a shovel
Scraping up a shock or a swatch of dirty snow?
For different reasons is an old man old,
Do women munching peppermints
Pass below our heated rooms bluing in the cold.
Wasn't Charlottesville a wonder for us all,
T. Peter, when drunk, in arms, at night
Howling Hopkins, we stumbled down the mall?
We know too well the whining for the nice things
And just how swell we clutch our sugar-stick;
Our endless bookish meals bring, of course,

The justified desserts we suck and lick,
And we've been taught to do this well,
Chewing flavor from the nutmeats close to burning logs.
Oh, it's not the impish tricking, no, dear, no
Or your thousand goofy smiles
Which defines for me a yell,
And not the sick professor, either, staring through
The well-rubbed panes of ancient glass
As he watches all the ice-cold shivers
That run through the frozen dogs.
Simply, that's the nutstone moulding on the grass;
A swift corroding of the liver rakes
And insult to the brain is also swift:
The history of sunstarts on a lake,
A quivering octave of a quivering note.
Buried in a yell, however, is something from the throat.
Not the bung-stopped clotting in the bedroom,
Neither noises in the lotions nor good-byes,
And not the oafish sucking noises of the fingers,
Nor the sad, sad giggling sound that lingers
In the holy, holy eating clubs, the hooting and the doom
(the terror of watching people's eyes)
Mother Red Cap's darlings, Old Dad's ploys
Who chuckle at things phallic
And know so little of so much soundless noise.
And there: the never-car that waits metallic,
Shiny gold it waits, under its hot drops
(If I mention Universities
Should I put them in italic?)
For the countless little fops,
Moist and ready from their baths,
Ready to die like the jelly monster
With a piteous glug, but without his wrath.
But if you listen there's the yell,
The mandrake shriek, the cough of a goat;
Buried in a yell is something from the throat
Which makes a tumor of the horn,
Like an old man in Corfu warning waves,
A fish-eye on the deep,
The howl of a God who ripens corn,
Rusts iron, and now begins to rave.
Can a God denied, neglected, utter this old scorn?

And what's the yell, the howl, the shriek
That's buried down inside?
The exasperated long, long sigh
In the throat of the yell
Just for the listener in his private hell
To tell us God has died.

The Harvard College Tinies

1

O Swung Tree,
Your servant oranges
Hang from you,
Terrified.

2

Do you love me
Or do you not?
You told me once
But I forgot.

3

Corpses are buried,
Cadavers un-;
The distinction's pointless
In terms of fun.

4

Girls have mothers
Upon their backs to bite 'em,
So girls grab boys
And so ad infinitum.

5

A lexical man came to marry
And erred for the trull's mood did vary.
The rosy-cheeked bride, feared a
Uxoricide.
Prevail, sturdy man, through the parry.

6

Holy Divine Providence
Did one thing odd;
Allowed a cruel absurdity
The name of God.

7

In wordly law as it is built
He was innocent of guilt.
Explain now the nature of this offense:
He was guilty of innocence.

8

The piece of foolscap
By a poem enhanced
Is never completed;
It's only advanced.

9

Of the two main reasons why earth exists,
Walking on it is one, says the prophet;
But among his number you needn't enlist.
So proceed, dear friend, to walk off it.

Harvest Time

Autumnal days make me believe
There is in leafmeal musk, apple smells,
A mood of something like prevision.
Yesterday kicking through the leaves
I brought a bottle of wine
As a gift over to my new neighbors,
A lovely young couple who knew I was a writer
(How? All my books are out-of-print).

It suddenly struck me walking home
Reflecting on their grateful grace
That given the small celebrity I have,
The kind in my village that goes for something
But not of course too much,
They'd one day be at my funeral.

Haves and Holes

Like a novel, like a sequel,
Marriage is that equal:
Halves, but one half previous,
The other, somewhat devious,
A counterpart, say, in the following way:
As a workweek equals a Friday's pay.
Two stones grind in an ancient quern;
One stays static, one will turn.
Nothing in nature is equal quite.
Jaws don't match in a single bite.
Your ear on the right, your ear on the left—
Some will say "reft," some will say "cleft":
The words to that queer inner porch both apply.
The cave from the darkness who can descry?
The terms are the same, but not so the ear,
With shapes as different as smiles from tears.
A push, you say, is only a pull?
A glass half empty is a glass half full?
The riddle's the riddle of number two;
The one call me, the other you.
But a couple, alas, is not a pair.
Love's disappointment's precisely there!
If a simple kiss is what one wants,
Turning the cheek is the other's response.
The vision you'd share can never be,
Not to another who cannot see.
For the singular act of creation
Absolves the other of obligation.
Love letters sent, countless and grand,
Parch the pen in the other's hand.
The fair, they say, requires foul;
An owl is cognate to its howl.
And if with love you see your fate,
Why, be prepared to suffer hate!
In the duchess you wooed at the midnight hour
Claws a black-faced bitch mad to devour.
You seek to select and select what you see,
But is what appears what then must be?
The nature of choice *itself* is sin,
Where one must lose and one must win!

One eye's inaccurate, two we need
To watch, to learn, to know, to read.
One image is gotten of those two:
But is it real? And is it true?
Distinctions! Differences! All life long!
You can't do right if you can't do wrong.
The bride, the groom on a nuptial bed?
Spills one white, spills one red.
Yet each fulfills defect in each,
The epistemology of stone and peach.
(But when it comes to the hungry lip,
Are equally praised, the flesh, the pip?)
A paradox, say, that can never be:
The strange conundrum of lock and key.
Man's "too much" he boasts to show;
Woman's "too little" down below
Incorporates as best it can
The larger half of her messmate, Man.
A larger half? Ay, there's the catch.
It's the deathless quintessential,
The flint, the strike, the spark sequential,
That fires every human match.

History Is Made at Night

Deception is the price too many pay for love.
A knife beneath the tongue, a vow above
As thin as lies,

Lost to whatever dreams when young it hoped to find,
In innocence it sought to bind
With honest ties.

How can ever love transform a soul, redeem
A spirit unalert to all but its own scream
Of greed?

The self that fights for gain itself is fought,
Content to fill its own and not
Another's need.

There are plots as red as witches in our heart,
Turning love to schemes, and schemes impart
A living blight.

A blackness that infects us soon can make us shade.
I think what's often said is true: history is made
At night.

The Hollywood Rag

Hand me my populuxe hat,
Give me my rancho mirage cane,
Sing me a parody, instant hilarity,
I've got a yen to be vain.
O, O, O pink villas and palms,
Sweet baby, open your arms,
Doing the Hollywood Rag.

Put on your Malibu tails,
Don your flamingo beak shoes,
Drive me nutty, turn me to putty,
Tell me only good news.
O, O, O pink villas and palms,
Sweet baby, open your arms,
Doing the Hollywood Rag.

Make up your insincere face,
Wear silver earrings that peal,
Wing me a wing, fling me a fling,
Let's try and pretend to be real.
O, O, O pink villas and palms,
Sweet baby, open your arms,
Doing the Hollywood Rag.

Kick up those art deco feet,
Extend your clicquot club arm,
Let's be tacky, drive me wacky,
Turn on your boulevard charm.
O, O, O pink villas and palms,
Sweet baby, open your arms,
Doing the Hollywood Rag.

I Think of Death at Times

I think of death at times,
I mean my own, the one
I dream of and wake up
choking on a dry tongue,
wish for when the woof's
too tight and nerves snap,
whiplash, tangle at the
edges of my moving frame.

Sometimes on summer days (I am alone),
lying in the snap,
lying in the sand, all life
cooked out of me except
a violent consciousness,
I plan the whole affair,
or try to, but never get
beyond the crusty scene of Wiglaf
sprinkling water on my
beautiful face.

If Love Is the Licking and Tugs at the Movies

For Mimi

If love is the licking and tugs at the movies,
  it's also the thing that puts kids there,
Gaping and buttery in the hundreds rows are friends
  of us, let us say, plenty of kiddos who,
Lumped with sweetened drinks and sticky gums,
  crouch in the dark and know, because they are,
    the mystery of love.

Then there's the cranking and the grainy sounds
  that, like splicing moms and dads, join together
And throw flashing blacks and whites beyond their eyes,
The gleeful little bunnies who race into the loge
  and, funny, peep and poke among their origins.

The beefy curtains and the crazy dark, the oyster eye
  high up in the back like God's they are always
Ready to begin with things, crack open the day
  with marching songs and bags of provision for all.

And row upon row of heads, some like jezail bullets,
  some like puddings, burst with clicks and shouts;
Jamming their thumbs into popcorn, the squeaking only
  dies when the filing out begins. And the
Tubby wonders and the filthy-haired children know
  just where they've been
When it's time for the squinting sunlight, when
  the confections spread sick in the rib.

All the wet licked papers and the apple sticks
  chewed by attrition and booted down the aisle,
The gauze and lemon balls that are knotted in the rug,
  remain but more explain
    the racing in tomorrow of newer generations,
    grinning, walleyed, freckled, and sneaky,
The newest popeyed lovers of celluloid and life.

And all the drumbeats and the music,
   all the tinsel, hugging, licking and the rest
   is more, and don't be silly, than
Ho-hos in the dark; it's the zigzagging and the whim,
   of those who will love out, and
Those who were loved in.

Iliad

We all heard the mad birds
Telling us to kill
Our loves
With murders and by schemes
Unheard of since Achilles
Broke Hector's spine in thirds;
Sing out a wild adeste
To those very birds
Who shriek bent songs,
For who denies the questions
Will be answered
By the dreams we have of Priam,
The lovely graces of his and our
Beautiful faces,
Our winking jewels,
The deaths
And small, but real,
Resurrections.

Imagos

What I thought
the most wonderful
butterfly I had ever seen,
daubed double, yellow, white,
winged, shuttling straight up,
and from flower to flower,
was, when I came
close, two.

Insect

So awful is the vice of incest that no noun exists for the person who practices it.

—Alexander Theroux

What would you do
If your sister once said
Visiting you

That your brother
Tried to take her to bed,
Tell another?

To *someone* you
Must find yourself led.
My question is who?

In the Children's Parks Is Fun

In the children's parks is fun
But more than that a pleasant motion.
When the squeaky rubber ducks are pushed
Beneath the water up they come.
The little girls like pencils
Know what the slide delivers
When from the top the shove brings down
Like a golden puff of pistol
A little tyke, all coos and stripes.
The kite that jerks with bastardy
Up in the air with ughs and swoops
Will have fell tomorrow
And wasn't up there yesterday.
Look at the swings, they're back and forth,
A rolling roiling motion;
The kiddies know when it goes south
It then has to go north.
The kiddies bounce in the frosty air
At the balance, but there's more:
If a creature's ripped from a momma's womb,
A papa must go to war.

Job

Where are the truths you wanted to hear
But couldn't for the lies the doubters told?
Though Bildad called you guilty, Eliphaz queer,
In the face of all destruction you stood bold.
The promise made, that He that keepeth Zion
Should not slumber, should not even sleep,
A faith emboldened strong enough to die on,
Gave a faithless nation promises to keep.
Now, Israel itself is lost once more,
A persecutor in the very way it hurt,
Tells the very lies it only heard before,
Grinds another nation in the dirt.
Why ask again the ways of God, His mystery?
Palestine's impaled on Israel's history.

Joni James

Nobody could love you
For yourself and not your voice.
My own angel couldn't have
Stranger, more beautiful diction
In her song, though my choice
When I meet her in the sky
Is that she try.

La Compagnie idéale

Pressant,
A demi-submergé,
Monte sous notre vie
Un désir de compagnie idéale.
Ce désir n'est pas l'idée
Qu'existe telle compagnie;
It est cette compagnie.
J'avoue que peu m'importe
De rester assis a observer le monde
Si le monde ne m'importune;
J'ajoute que jamais je n'ai trouvé
De compagnie
D'aussi bonne compagnie que
Le solitude qui donne forme
A ce désir, et donc,
Pour l'essentiel,
A moi-meme.

Perfect Companion

An urge
Beneath our life
Is the half-submerged wish
For a perfect companion.
The wish is not the notion
A companion can be had;
It's the companion.
I can say, I don't mind
Sitting and watching the world without
The world bothering me.
I can add, I've never found
A companion
As companionable as
The solitude that makes
The wish, and so me,
Much of what
I am.

Le Bruit

Noise is the most impertinent form of interruption.

—Schopenhauer

Take those Dadaists with frying pans.
Le bruit with its banging tins and horns,
Typewriters, rattles, kettledrums, and bells

Shook awake the capital of Paris.
So, a table's not its wood and nails
But, as you say, the mere idea of it.

O Tzaraites, you're something premature,
For isn't noise produced by every movement?
The soul itself in nature is volcanic,

The very opposite of what theologians
With their platitudes of Plato claim,
That we in being virtuous must be quiet.

But what in a person awake's to be approved
Whose vitality announces little but that
Noise is rich? Chocolate will kill a dog.

I prefer girls doing elegant bascules
In silence, shimmering like the sh-sh-sh-sh
Of the silver leaves of the poplars,

The secret thoughts they hide to harbor,
Dreaming, the manias of moans they save
For silken beds they plan to quiver in.

Little League Parents

Squinting into the sun,
You both watch from afar,
Bellowing for the team in the field
Wearing blueberry blue,
Eating fistwiches, wedges of pie,
The carboy of lemonade nearby
Gone warm by inning two.
Your screams at little peewee
In right, wearing his hat down low,
Can't compensate for the fact
He's whiffed three times in a row.
You're spread out on a hummock
Like Litvaks on a beach.
Good that that fucking umpire
Is conveniently out of reach.
Smoking butts one after another
From the pack perched on your knee,
Isn't your face-shaking fury
Exactly what half-pints shouldn't see?
Aren't you as badly out-of-shape
As your anger is, as unpromising
A parent to fumbling Freddy
As his bat angle is to me?
And when I see you waddling
Moose-slow into dusk
With your lawn chairs
Across those empty fields,
I wonder, can anyone doubt
Specifically how
Beyond here and now
That little boy struck out?

The Lollipop Trollops

Matsu, spread out your netsukes.
A good one has no sharp points.
It can't. And it must also stand.

What in any particular arrangement
Doesn't show to the derelict mind,
Capable of missing what it sees,

Patterns forcing thought on us,
As the past exists to be summoned,
Painful as points and placement?

The poet is a veteran of the night,
Method the soul of his management,
Drawing lines that you might dream,

Indeed surrender to your dreams
But not without the working mind
Sharply shaped about its themes.

Knowledge isn't often what you like.
It may by truth more than in disguise
Surprise a tragic shadow in your eyes.

A poem must teach, as a blowing wind
After constant rain manages somehow
To bring summer somehow in again,

But along with birds a bleaching heat
Against which we must interpose of course
White sombreros and cold umbrellas.

Praise enough for sunny Solomon.
David having lessons in his wrists
Sang twice in giving sense to song.

* * *

But poetry should please as well.
Blow your fat trumpet, senator,
To those didacticians at your feet

Who've given up magic and shadow,
Becoming eunuchs for the jobs they want.
"I've been too harsh on Brother Donkey,"

Cried Saint Francis on his dying bed.
His spirit needed pleasure, too.
Rip off your sleeves in spring!

Isn't high seriousness for sects?
Mormons don't want masques, pinwheels,
Silly cats, noisy flats, party hats.

As trollops singing "Zuk Zuk Zuk!"
Heedless as their clients are un-,
Poems to that extent are fun.

Forgive the painted trulls in heels
If only for the sad disclosures they
In hocks of laughter are intent to hide.

A simple lyric makes us as unaware
Of time as time is of itself in passing.
Can't sense be made of only what we feel?

The pleasure that we seek in them
And often find makes poems like boxes
Lovely as Italian bijouterie.

Jubilo! Jubilo! Jubilo!
Skip into sheets of driving rain with me
So we can lick our faces and laugh!

* * *

But who remains the same
After no matter how little knowledge makes
Of us as much a mood as a man?

A different cowpoke
Walks out of a crepuscular cathedral
Than who went strolling in

By definition. What indirection
That you seem to take, squandering time,
Fails to matter? None, *none.*

We are never twice ourselves.
Whether read for sensuality or sense
A poem must disturb,

Badly reminding you, spintry
And spintressa, of your need to be
Surely more than what you are.

Smug students, reading to have
Themselves confirmed, ignore or wave away
Despair like ditzy drones,

Refusing to see we progress
Precisely by what low logo of misfortunes
We are willing to face

And face to know, like Alexander
In Tashkurghan, rousing himself from bed
To survey the hostile hills,

Leaving in a sweaty pile of pelts
At way past midnight alert to sudden danger
A naked and disturbed Roxane.

Lost Friend

Most of him recalled for me
One of Puddn'head Wilson's remarks,
Which were rarely kind,
Although they got a laugh.
"I wish I owned
Half of that dog," he said.
"I'd kill my half."
Why form friendships
Over which one must then reluct?
I once knew a guy
Who though some of him
Was nice
Much too much of him
Sucked.

Lost in America

I searched for you in Critical, Mass.,
Won't, Wash., and Eightnine, Tenn.,
Over every last road and mountain pass
Of Lo, Cal., and Ball Point, Penn.

You went skipping about in Tra La, La.,
In each suburb and city park
Of the palmy reaches of Flip Flop And, Fla.,
Junior, Miss., and Noah's, Ark.

Doctors were called in Chekhov, Md.,
Ex, Conn., and spacious Big, Al.,
Pro Nobis, Ore., and Ravish, Me.,
And the deserts of Silent, Cal.

Eeny, Meeny, Miny, Mo.,
Seemed a logical place you'd be in.
Same with dark Agememnon, Io.,
Either, Or., and Waita, Minn.

You rented a car in Miner, Va.,
Uncaring that you were remiss,
And took as you sped out of Areyou, Ok.,
A motel in Nowmakea, Wis.

Racing through Luc, Ky., one night in snow
You decided you wanted to try
To avoid my pursuit by trying to go
From Pho, N.Y., to Dontaskme, Wy.

You tried Salaam, Al., had nothing to see.
Then apparently traveled as far
As the lawless outbacks of Givitto, Me.,
And freezing Looknohands, Ma.

Who was it saw you in Do Re, Mi.?
One newspaper in Valhal, La.,
Had you living half naked up in a tree
Drooling in rural Ga, Ga.

You were never quite right after the day,
Or so went the rumor mill,
You spent two weeks on a fatal stay
In Suddenly Taken, Ill.

Gossip quickly had you trans-
Ferred to a living hell,
A barmy house in Bottles And, Kans.
Some whispered in Infi, Del.

Enough of this crazy fantasia about
What sounds like a chronic disease.
Allegorical paranomasia! Watch out
For accompanying medical fees!

I despair, do you hear, because I have landed
No closer than when I'd begun.
I'm doomed I see to stay where I'm stranded
In the terrible state of the pun.

Love, 1957

The only way
I could like her
Was to feel bad
About myself
After hating her.
The only way
I could make amends
For berating her
Was pitifully
To start dating her.
The only way
I could feel right
With myself
Was to marry her
After creating her.

Loverboy

"After the lovin',"
croons Engelbert Humperdinck,
"I'm still in love with you,"
as if it's a bloody miracle
in the process of getting through

he still can manage
to feel in his heart
for the woman lying unkempt
anything resembling love
and not just merely contempt;

but were I
that she to whom he sang
those crapulous words in bed
I'd sever his flaccid tool
And slap him around the head.

The Man with the Fenestrate Shoes

For Bettina Field Carroll

I remember, I remember still.
I felt the just sun in my bones,
the volumes underneath my arm,
and watched the symptoms of a grin
on the spooning cook's face
for the girl from Fiesole I loved
who could be read on me
as I walked and walked and walked.
The brown lace of the Arno
flowed through my beautiful soul.
Today, oh do the miraculous!
My bread felt good in my pocket;
the hand need only poke about
To feel the glory of the yeast,
flour, flowers, beaten, warm,
To be eaten near the water.
By the naked umber walls,
past men and churching women,
spiraling in peppermint,
alive, on wings, medicinal,
I pass in my hat, Assyrian cap,
speedy with my holy lunch,
giggling at the time on my hands,
almost guilty from my joy.
I was lighter than heartsong,
ready with my dream of lyrics
for the girl I leant less upon
than against the walnut trees
all afternoon above the city,
letting my fingers needle up
and down and softly all around
the sacrament of special moments
and felt the pentecosts promised
through the hole in my Italian shoes.

Mary Snowfire

All the boys knew Mary Snowfire,
Who wore lipstick at thirteen and a pout,
More than by the Ping-Pong photos
Snapped half in a booth, half out.
At night she dawdled at Webster Park.
"I see France," she once said.
Of the heat that so held me in thrall
For others who smirked in the dark
Though my life was cold as December
No whisper fails to enter my head
And most of those girls I somewhat recall
With a memory not always up to the mark,
But Mary Snowfire I remember.

We slicked down our hair with Vitalis
To dance in the gym at the junior high
Where Miss Bigwood kept us an arm apart
And we avoided contact by eye.
I waltzed in silence with Shirley and Clare
In my boxlike shoes and I ached,
Never quite knowing to stop or start.
I had combed and wet-parted my hair.
A number of girls I knew from the hall
With breath sweeter than birthday cake
Brought a blush to my cheek like an ember
And many a one of them I can recall
To whom I'd have given all of my heart,
But Mary Snowfire I remember.

Medford Kids

He combed his hair, proud,
    and,
        with large fat sighings,
    dillydallied about.

She took out a Lucky
        and tapped it on his
            arm.

Furious with each other,
    they kissed, lovely.
    He with his pomade;
        She with her funny
            truncheon.

The Meeting of the Heads

The meeting of the heads with eyes
Prevents the murder love attempts.
There are the perfect fingers
Lovers use, the snatches in the dark.
And it's awfully brave of some
To pile on lovely in the sheets
When murder smells out loud for them.
No, not the glugs of life passing out,
The quimmy tugging of the gluey sheets,
Is it we should think about;
But the ripe wet daggers that commit
Along with hugs, our heads.
Then the eyes: acrobating like feathers,
These are the pouncing things,
Hopping beyond the mammaries, and
Even the slope of chin and armatures;
Cellulose or beady, likable or red,
It's the eyes the head brings soft to love,
Walleyed and warranteed, like eggs,
To crack and flutter and spill.

Megabucks Ticket

A winning Megabucks ticket worth three-quarters of a million
dollars, taken out at the Swan River Market in Dennis but never
picked up, was invalidated today, one year after being purchased.
—*Cape Cod Times,* June 19, 1991

"Your thermocouple's broke,"
The plumber muttered,
Face up in the cellar
Dark and cluttered,
Grunting, clucking, exhaling sighs
Under the water heater,
Getting cinders in his eyes.
"Got a scrap of something
On you I can light?"
"I might," came the helpful reply,
"I might."

Mens Sana in Corpore Sano

Dr. Nathan Pritikin
Who told Jim Fixx, "Take heed.
Stop eating meat;
Your veins are clogged
And running doesn't help
Unclog them,"
Was right of course,
But when he died—
Nate, I mean (who shot
Himself in the head)
Not Jim (who jogging
Fell down dead)—
His veins were clear
As a twelve-year-old's.
Only his *mind* was clogged.
How many the miles
His spirit never logged?
So much for hopes.
Weightlifters never read.
Professors
Are physical dopes.

Milagro

Why cut your braids
in Quito, brown girl,

when others with hope
to win their loves

offer Santa Niño
in his shadowy niche

old medallions,
sacred vows paid,

of bone wood stone
gold shell clay?

O, give up your
tiny tin heart

to El Niño, girl,
in whatever way,

but never those
long dark braids.

Mill Stream

What is the secret said
In what unable to be held
We love? Spillways, pools,

The sea itself. Water moving
Has become for me, as much
As for Heraclitus in his mind,

While somehow proving,
The symbol of mutable beauty,
Masquerade as performance,

Form transcending flux.
Why can't flowing water,
Above its supernal duty,

Beyond its natural task,
Stop briefly meandering
Long enough for us to ask

May we *ever*, standing far above
The heart of what its secret says,
Come to hold what we love?

The Miracle of Fasting

Fasting makes a face that lights an onion up.
Three days without a morsel turns the stomach

Out as if it were a limp and laundered sock,
Scrimp and empty as a Dutchman's bummock.

I have often tried to supplicate my soul
By concluding that the body I was given

Is the worthless brute I know it is.
For mastery of self I long have striven.

Fat forces flesh to fast in cutting ways.
Fasts cut through fat and flesh obeys.

The hours drag. You're white as paper,
Can smell a pie some forty miles away.

If melons were a woman you would rape her;
For a tart in any sense you'd pay.

Our stupid flesh can never comprehend
How deprivations elevate our being.

Fatness is in fact a kind of blindness.
And fasting but a special way of seeing.

Monsieur Trinquet

O red-wigged wit from Tambov,
Everyone's favorite poet,

You came with the family Harlikov,
sponging at the name-day party

like all poets full of pride
content to let the others pay,

and danced with their spinster
daughter out of obligation.

Not a word that was recorded
did you exchange with Onegin,

that we know of. In your one
appearance you sang off-key,

worrying about your stanza
with an aesthetician's fears.

I only want to know was Tatiana
Larin as beautiful as they say,

Or were you too busy to notice,
Filling your face with eclairs?

Moses the Lawgiver

We give our word to the Palestinians we want peace.
                    —Yitzhak Shamir, Prime Minister of Israel

Moses murdered a man, flat out,
Though this was against the law.
He saw an Egyptian, took up a knout,
And left him without a jaw.

Then Yahweh announced "Do not steal."
Try guessing who first got the news.
But did Moses believe what he had to reveal
Of the law he passed on to the Jews

When during the course of several nights,
Preceding the Exodus bold,
Egypt was robbed by the Israelites
Of its jewelry, silver, and gold?

Look in vain for a sign of remorse
After the thieves got the boot.
The Golden Calf was fashioned of course
From mostly Egyptian loot.

Another commandment was then handed down
To Moses who waited in dread
On a misty mountain above the town.
"Don't bear false witness," it said.

So Moses spoke up to Pharaoh
And his very first *word* was a lie.
Knowing full well he'd never come back,
He promised that he would try.

A very short leave was requested
For the people of Israel dear
To pray, have a feast, and get rested
In a wilderness really quite near.

What later of Moses' assurance
The feast would last only three days?
Or the worth of a prophet's endurance
Who can break laws in so many ways?

His word was as barren as sand.
What honor to all kith and kin!
They stole every valuable and
Their asses were gone with the wind.

One moral's as good as another
Of the many there are to be had.
Laws are made only for others.
Whatever you do can't be bad.

If Scripture's literal, anything goes.
Crime often pays. Laws are pied.
Savagery's sanctity fighting your foes
If you boast God on your side.

Rules without any exceptions
Are basically written for saps.
Truth depends on deception.
Another commandment perhaps?

One fact is undoubtedly certain
If you must call Moses a saint.
You view him through a gauze curtain
And persist on seeing what ain't.

That, and, however you pose it
If you still deny Moses a sinner,
History, as any fool knows it,
Is written, in fact, by the winner.

Mother Gideon

Once my god we allow for accusations
    Watch out for things female and dirt brown,
The terror stance that ducks us under bridges,
    Puffing and white with swollen feet.
The pipewife, Mother Gideon, in my nightmare
    Cabbaging her way through forests
Grimly held her torch and wolf for me.
    What of what she spies infuriates her face?
It's the truancy she hates, she do,
    Your failure as a member to erect
Underneath your braided spread. She looks.
    You have spread out all your comic books.
With a vicious pointed stick accusing
    She has waited for a boy who died.
Or so she said, moving toward your bed.
    Isengrim the wolf snaps terrified.
She wore a stocking cap of medieval brown,
    Burrowing toward you in her circus clothes.
Hideously, she was what most you feared
    For accusing her of what you felt
By dreaming of a mother with a wolf
    Who seemed about to kill you
In the way people said you were born.

Mrs. Mixter

And what judgement would step from this to this?
—Hamlet

"She's really not a bad sort,"
Someone who knew her once said,
"And yet" (a pause for this report)
"Married four times!"
It left a vivid picture in my head.
The beautiful is *one,*
Presents itself as unity,
Fullness, not community,
Chooses, is, has done.
The ugly is multiple. Life
Nourishes the whole,
As a husband should a wife;
Oneness is the beauty of the soul.

Why speak of parts that never fit,
Messiness as neatness?
Not divided, separate, or split,
Beauty is completeness.
Ugliness betrays degrees.
If the ugly were complete
(The way soul and body meet)
Without a trace of beauty,
It would for that very reason
—By definition and by duty—
Cease to be ugly, discrete,
To itself a treason:
A woman who weds once,
And not in every season.

Mussolini

The mob loves strong men. The mob is a woman.

—Benito Mussolini

You loved to strut,
Made your buttocks even wag,
Though you stood no more than 5'6"
Searching the crowd,
Looking for a girl to shag.
They were one and the same,
You say, easy to conquer,
Being easy to sway.
You shaved your head
To look like Caesar,
Saw yourself above the pope.
But was that really you?
When you curled your lip,
Wooing women to your bed,
Scowling, head flung back,
Didn't that aloofness
Indicate far less cunning
Than a low IQ?
Braced on your feet,
Hands on your hips,
Standing in your scarlet Alfa,
Romeo, your peasant face
Mahogany dark, livid lips,
Bulbous with a cretin's eyes,
Your lantern jaw thrust out,
Completing a lump,
Half provolone, half melanzana,
Who but a woman
Could fall for that?
But if what makes a mob
Makes a woman, as you say,
Women give tit for tat.
So why expect less passion
From those harpies, moulinyan,
Who strung you up like ragusano
In that piazza in Milan?
And when lifting up their skirts

♦ 109 ♦

They urinated on your upturned face,
Which they squatted just above,
Why bother to deny,
With what you know of mobs
And how they're just
Like women,
It had less to do with love?

The Night of the Niffelheim Dwarfs

For Steven Moore

There were cobblers, cocktails, white cups, and flips
    Neguses, nectars, and wet juleps.
And out danced the dwarfs in a dance so true.
    O, that night on the sward the sward was blue,
    For blue is the sward at night.

There were sangarees, nectars, shrubs, and slings,
    Smashes, catawbas, and Bimbo stings,
Around hopped the dwarfs in their nighties new.
    O, that night on the sward the sward was blue,
    For blue is the sward at night.

There were liquors, absinthes, and blood red ports,
    Toddies, mulls, and arrack orts,
Through their magic cheeks the dwarfs then blew.
    O, that night on the sward the sward was blue,
    For blue is the sward at night.

There were brandies, drams, and sputtering nogs,
    Juniper gins and buttered grogs,
From the fire leaped a girl of heavenly hue!
    O, that night on the sward the sward was blue,
    For blue is the sward at night.

There were ching-chings, malts, and spiced radish ales,
    Fog-cutters, whiskeys, and bottled pales.
Then up on one dwarf their black crow flew.
    O, that night on the sward the sward was blue,
    For blue is the sward at night.

There were bishops, filled tumblers, and bitters queer,
    Mother Shiptons and bumbable beer,
"Marry her! Marry her!" the cruel bird crew.
    O, that night on the sward the sward was blue,
    For blue is the sward at night.

There were punches, brown mums, and bottle jack,
    Antique barley wine and poker-hot sack,
But what the dwarfs wanted the girl wouldn't do.
    O, that night on the sward the sward was blue,
    For blue is the sward at night.

There were clarets, grappa, flosters, and sops,
    Furious cognacs and worts with hops.
The dwarfs in a cluster all angry grew.
    O, that night on the sward the sward was blue,
    For blue is the sward at night.

There were perries, caudles, and cider nips,
    Black-stripe mixtures and calabash sips.
As the girl screamed in pain the dwarfs screamed, too.
    O, that night on the sward the sward was blue,
    For blue is the sward at night.

There were sifters, moonshines, and muscat casks,
    Aqua composita and barleycorn flasks,
The rejected dwarf's eyes grew scarlet with rue.
    O, that night on the sward the sward was blue,
    For blue is the sward at night.

There were meads, tall bourbons, sherries, and hock,
    Pitches, rosins, and murderous bock.
Then flashed a knife which one of them drew.
    O, that night on the sward the sward was blue,
    For blue is the sward at night.

There were squashes, tokays, and mystic stouts,
    Spirits of wormwood and devil-get-outs,
Their funeral grins shone through the night dew.
    O, that night on the sward the sward was blue,
    For blue is the sward at night.

Padre Todopoderoso

I am fat with vision,
A cleric transubstantiating hosts
With a hoc and a poc.

My creed is all things
Are to be seen to be understood
To be known, Scotus,

To be good. *Creador*
Del Cielo y de la tierra! Ink's a drug.
I have titquills, paper, hands

Strong as a fruit tramp's
To wield a pen to circumscribe
The fat round wholeness

Of the vast compossible.
Big jumanna! No fat blue marble
Is more real than dreams

And I am sitting one off
You at dinner, Sleepy and Dumbo,
Taking notes. Wake up!

Part of Loving's Leaving

For Patricia Mortellite

Part of loving's leaving,
Just as part of leaving's love;
For lovers part, it's right.
What's left is happening
Beyond belief or out of sight,
And yet between the loving:
The lover's word's parole,
A predictable control
That makes love's leaving
Loving just the same,
To word itself apart
Softly as a candle weaving
Carbon from a flame.
But know departure when it's there,
For up and down and north and south
And logically is built the stair;
The mystery that swings a door
Makes loving far or leaving near.
Yet words also mean parole;
Parole means that there's more
Of words, like flames
Within a burning coal.
We loving leave and leaving love;
Hello then, as it must,
Eventually becomes good-bye;
The harmony of fire and smoke
That joins the earth to sky.
There's down below and up above,
For part of loving's leaving,
Just as part of leaving's love.

Patriotic Bigots

Celebrate, America, and crow.
You've never been cursed
With being bombed
Or seen planes flying low.
I love the way big guys with guts
Talking in the post office,
Their faces like fists,
Cry, "We'll kick their butts."
"Bomb Baghdad,"
Sing the jingoists,
"Put it to the rack!"
Where did you ever see more
Of nothing?
The desert
Isn't only in Iraq.

Yellow-ribbon wearers
Approve as kin do kin
The flag fetishist
With his patriotic pin
Prominent upon his dress.
"They don't value life as
We do," said fat Marlin Fitzwater,
Speaking to the press.
"Bomb the A-rabs,"
Sing the jingoists,
"Scorch the bastards black!"
Where did you ever see more
Of nothing?
The desert
Isn't only in Iraq.

Passacaglia for an Italian Witch

For Camille

"I don't *do* blurbs!" you screech,
Howling, wagging your short dark arms,
Like some mad spaventapasseri.

Who the fuck are you, zoticona,
Strega with murderous mouth and mustache,
Ragout of draggled ideas,

Not to crow or cack or comment
When that's all, mortrewer of quips and quotes,
You're known for ever having done?

What's a carping critic but blather,
Boustrophedon, banter, bullshit, total blab?
Your rage is only sad flirtation.

Who more bitter than a lowbred crone
Writing words like plaiting rotten straw
Claiming it for either gold or art?

You're no more after privacy,
Vecchiacchia, than your foghorning fancies
Cry out to us to be ignored.

It's only in your ratty reveries,
In the muttering insistence of your mind
You're as important as your acolytes,

All five or six or so of them,
Laughably insist you must insist you are,
Middle-aged culture-humper!

What hideola of a critic with her bags
Of half-assed hoodoo can't be counted on for blurbs?
Aren't blurbs all you fucking do?

Pathology of War

Proclaim this, you people among the nations, "Sanctify war!"
—Joel 3:9

I have a certain sympathy with war,
It so apes the gait and bearing of the soul.
Murder fighting mercy is a kind of law.

The longing need to love that keeps us whole
Also summons what it can't abide,
For what we fear it from a part of manhood stole.

We fight to prove that we refuse to hide
The dog in us that gentleness rubs raw,
Lest what or whom we kiss the killer might deride.

To Henry D. Thoreau

Peasant Festival

In memory of Pieter Bruegel the Elder

The chunky little men turn red
Before we catch them in the act of ruin.
And when melodies blow forth on reeds,
The huffing red men surely love to hop.
Medieval times were full of woody halls
And breakfast girls in blue sailed in
With eggs and frothy pints
Before the men turned red.
Little kids in pie-wide hats
Ran around in crazy circles goosing cats,
The old men farted and the nuns sung by,
The pryncocks boys with poop and glee
Made themselves so windy and so round
We knew they had the lovey hugs that
Never needed love.
They toppled cards and yelled from faces
We are sad to lose, knowing well the men
Who reddened and swung like goats with tinny bells
To beefy-shaped violas and melon-headed girls.
I think about the hedge priest and his buzzardry,
The puffy trolls and trouncing elves
Who skipped on Whitsuns through the forests
And barged into their oyster wenches
And globe-titted wives and bouncing gammers:
They tongued them who ran quilly through the snow
In the pudding of their socks,
Remembering their mother's dugs, the velvet paps
That now their grinning moms forgot.
These were the chunky dancing men I saw,
The tubby sons of square-thumbed grannies
Who weaned the dirty shitter louts,
Able thumpers who grew waxy and as bold
As ax-headed woodmen can
And brothers in the knolls of green and Flanders—
Thorny in eye, heavy-waisted baronbums who rose
At night and gnawed the brains of sleeping cows
And skipped to the midnight pipes and reddened.
They hit with slingshots birds

And slept on hair. On pots they rolled;
They flailed things and never jammed their pewter
Pints on wood until they laughed with Jesus,
Hard, with prickling jokes and huge.
So hopping was the game, to trilling notes,
To silly yelling into winds,
In baggy pants and greasy caps,
They leap for us with springing heads
And then we see the men turn red
Before we catch them ruined.

Phantom of Werther

The question we ask of death is a fair question.

—Theroux, in drink

With his pistols
Werther must have wondered,
Having just been spurned,
If water thrown on fire
Isn't firstly burned;
And faced with that
Craziest of crazy dooms
Which of which
Initially consumes.

Pimp

As a literary agent
you hustle books like flesh,
A working burke for money,
an English snob in a coat,
2 percent castle, 98 moat.

The difference between
the preening you and a pimp,
since both of you are frauds,
when the arithmetic is done,
Is simple: there isn't one.

Poem for a Christening

The new soft bells tune in anew
Your child, a yawn and able arms,
To pass a dream,
The whole earth through:
Let the water be as much a kiss
As blessing;
The whispered prayers the lute
Which brings to consciousness
The loves and yes
We have, we've had;
And the salt reminder that a dream,
Small Tarquin,
Is often lost, is often sad.
So, if and when you're far from home,
Unfold, re-read,
And try to understand
The whole earth through
The meaning of
The bells and prayers and salt
You find again
In this poem I wrote for you.

A Poem in Which Is a Celebration by Negation
or, a repartee on jeopardy

If on a friend's bookshelf
You cannot find Joyce or Sterne
Cervantes, Rabelais, or Burton,

You are in danger, face the fact,
So kick him first or punch him hard
And from him hide behind a curtain.

Prayer for Manon

Composed on the Occasion of Her Birth, July 31, 1991

Grow, lovely child,
May the blessings
Of your birth adorn
Like sunlight
The whispering few years
We have. Be as true
No matter what may come
As on the day
That you were born.
Our span is short.
We pencil our names
On the membrane of a drum,
So brief is life, Manon.
Know only in the future
Lies the splendid memory
Of what your parents,
In their love,
Hope for you to understand
Of grace and beauty.
Follow that precept
Out of love, not duty.
Let your honor,
Like a medallion
Pure as the love
Conceiving you,
Be a measure of intent,
Sustain your joy,
Reflect your innocence,
That happiness,
Like rain, like song,
May fall across your life,
And all your dreams,
Manon, forever long,
Forever long.

Provincetown Chat

How can a sex
With an entrance
No matter how one directs it
Choose not to be willing
To oblige another
With such
A convenient exit?

When has sex
Please tell me
Even in places of lenience
Been ever aligned
To a process
With something
Approaching convenience?

The Raven

A parody written as a requirement for election to the
distinguished Raven Society at the University of Virginia, 1967

Twice within the week so given, to this assignment was I driven,
To fulfill my obligation to a curious *per favor.*
I was forced, despite resistance, with a curious insistence,
Not at all unlike persistence, a persistence I deplore.
"Write a parody," they muttered, "with subsistence, that's your chore."
Nothing more was added, and I murmured what a bore.

Now you may think it craven that I want to be a Raven,
But a member of the working class I've always been.
So with little exhortation, and as little information
To inform this incantation, I began my recitation
Like the Jingle Man who did it way back when.
People laughed. I didn't care a yen.

There seemed no need for muses or any of the magic juices
Which the poet sometimes needs to make him budge.
Everything was effervescence, a massive bundle of excrescence,
But my lack of phosphorescence
Made me seem, like Poe, a poet of sheer fudge.
I ran madly toward Parnassus, and then had to trudge.

My lines bunched like tangled rigging, me a madman madly digging,
Talking, mocking, wigging, jigging
In a strangely private kind of semaphore,
But I continued at my scribbling, an eighth-rate Poesque sibling,
And I thought of Rudyard Kipling
As the poem did everything but march up to the fore.

A verb, a noun, a bit of chatter, nothing, nothing seemed to matter,
For in the poem the clatter just became a thrum.
There wasn't an epiphany, or even good polyphony,
It was a breakfast without Tiffany.
The trick's to sing, the trick is not to hum,
Which is how you tell a poet from a bum.

So I sit above my verses with a maximum of curses,
  Suffering reverses I never thought I'd know.
And somehow it's demeaning to try to impose meaning
  On a fowl so overweening
As this silent upstart crow.
  For a poem with such a subject is an arrow sans a bow.

The nightingale of Keats was the greatest of his feats,
  And Shelley's skylark always meets with great aplomb,
And my heart has always stirred for Yeats's golden bird,
  But what strange brand of emetic did Poe use in his aesthetic
By working up a storm
  In getting so athletic, and then to write a bomb.

The waterfowl of Bryant was a perfect little client,
  And the albatross defiant came on the scene as something new.
But Edgar's bird can't hold a smidgeon to Coleridge's pigeon
  Or that symbol of religion
That Gerry Hopkins sent up in the blue.
  For these, ah these, yes these are all too few.

Sorrento has its doves and they fly so high above,
  And Noah doubtless loved his bird of peace.
But to make a sweet mosaic on a bird so damned prosaic
  Is like singing of Passaic
And that city's flocks of oily geese.
  But to the poem, that I might find release.

Our feathered friends are nice, for eating they suffice,
  For Thanksgiving, with some spice, they'll get the nod.
But shouldn't some propriety in this august society
  Allow for more sobriety?
So that we find more justifiable reward,
  Next time make the subject matter—God.

Reveries of Children Dying

I poked about for friends in winter,
    was blinded in my pajamas by the moon-man,
Blinked lucky at the icicles,
    jagged and Norwegian like skis.

The carnival wheel had sparks along
    its cutting edge, and blue-honed gears;
Midgets leaped for their private toys,
    like fireworks ignited from the ground.

Zap was the noise of my fist in the chocolate box,
    done in daisies like my clown hat.
It's the wet mouth of the trumpet, we remember,
    and the arrowhead of doughnut in the drawer.

Was I different to expect the story of a cow forever?
    The rubber in my shoes began to sicken me,
Like the awfully funny print of Joseph in his coat,
    giggled off by his brothers for a hole.

There are the cracked and pointing shoes, out,
    beneath my room, smelling like iodine marks,
I dreamt of jelly baskets full of threads and needles,
    the hint of a French horn down the street.

It was as much my roasting oatmeal bowls, piping,
    as the endless pocketful of snow,
And the misery cones I nibbled in the park,
    that gladdened me beyond measure in my chair.

We all have for dreams the mild susurrus of the babies,
    the inchlings placed in rows like blackboard chalk,
Its fumes too, and the lilac of our teacher
    who took attendance in the darts of rain.

Silent and foxy but mild, we spilled onto the floor
    each peg of language; my socks were green that day,
When I thought in the mirror: Was it for me to march
    into the kitchen and demand a cookie?

I received my red and orange fife for Christmas,
  the fat pencil I was bound to give away.
Laughing, I tugged at the plastic fruit
  and imaginatively left for the stairs.

We hold our breath and try with delicacy to touch
  our fathers, there in shouts and hair,
Eating lunches at the foot of cellars,
  I loved the way I held his hand by the finger.

I walked on treetops fashioned from my dreams,
  as real as most of them promised to become.
Every night through starlit eyes I saw
  obedient to me, my bath, and my bready mother.

Then my pastel book I knew, and Christiana,
  dimpled in her leggings and her gold,
Walked me through the windmill,
  never startled at my footsteps.

No one seemed home when I had my nickel-plated dimes,
  the counting silver on the gum-colored magazines;
I watched for treasures in the meadow
  And was more than glad with my Crunch bars, and my soup.

A muffled shout from the pantry made me stop immediately;
  sighing in my flannel shirt my giggling friend
Beeped a nice hello, proving there was no dead child
  lying among the spices and the recipes.

First the penny on the counter, then the finger
  pointing through the glass.
We hear the door slam, but with our courage,
  march out with clucks and holding our sweet ribs.

It can't be called a gasp, but rather gasping:
  the pink of the nursery diminishes the squeak
Of terror, the wide-mouthed rage we have,
  too small, in knickers, as we look ahead.

Romard

What, sculptor, do you see
Within what's missing that
You have to mold to make,
Shaping thin from fat?

How does the hammer arm
Not lose the tender touch
In what it takes from life
To give to art so much?

Which transfigures better
Out of pain coming twice,
Adding, subtracting,
Chiseling fire, cutting ice?

Why is the fragile soul,
Burnt like molten steel,
Ignored by critics
In what it dares reveal?

Where goes the self,
Relieved of what it feels,
Giving to idle metal what
From the heart it steals?

Who is that strange enigma
Given the gift to make,
Artist consumed with fire
Or martyr burned at the stake?

Samoan Brother

You might think perhaps that a bully,
Not having grace, rising in his cockpit of bombast and fat
Like some tempestuous conductor with his haystack hair
To write you nasty letters, is not sentimental.
But no: he is a hog of tears and flowers
For his daughter, shallow wife, an aria or two,
Views of old Samoa, and is easily forgetful
At just such times and not regretful—
Or so is my surmise—when not punching someone blue
Or dreaming to, he feels good enough to eat
Something of his size.

Sarcastic Middle-aged Women

Don't they find their faces hatchets?
Are clawing and pawing all they know,
Sharp-elbowed cunts all they ever want to be?
Have they ever read a single book,
Prayed with their minds, knelt on stone
For no one but God above to see?
What frost is colder than their looks?
Are the muscles used to sing
The same used by women to give birth?
I only wonder why neither are popular
Among these pants-wearing tarts I know
With mustaches and mouths like chain saws
Muttering through their fucus and cigars,
"I love to break and tear. Beware!"

Six Limericks

When Charlene Pigg reads the news?
Man, it's Henry Mancini on blues.
   I don't mean to be harsh
   But call Jordan Marsh
And find her work fitting shoes.

You want a conception of dumb?
Take a pen the size of your thumb.
   Charlene's brain is as thin
   As the refill put in
With some added leeway to strum.

Charlene? A girl with an attitude,
Not the slightest conception of gratitude.
   But think of the strain
   Of having a brain
Beta-blocked with her kind of fatitude.

Let's buy Charlene a very strong anorak
To go string in faraway Kodiak
   Or cold Lackawanna
   With a helmut-cam on her
Or the stews of beleaguered Iraq.

For Charlene's replacement we choose
Anyone—the station can't lose.
   Just get a droolie
   To sit on a stoolie
And drawl, "This is the 10 o'clock news."

You want to buy Charlene a lariat,
A ring, say, some boots, or a chariot?
   Mail the woman the gift
   And you start a rift;
Your ass is intended to carry it.

Sneezes

Most compound consonantal sounds,
Odd to the eyes because taken from Greek,
We legitimately try to avoid on the grounds
Comprehending them takes more than a week.

Cnidoblast, Ptychodera, Bdellostoma,
Mnemotechnic, Xylem, Ctenophora

To pronounce such words next you are led,
With a nose that twitches as if smelling fescue,
And though you manage to get the word said,
The corresponding response is "God bless you!"

Acanthobdella, Gnathostomata, Psammobatis,
Cnemial, Zygaena, Pneumatophore

Snobbish Women at McDonald's

But you won't be seen there.
Where swaggarts eat? Where comedy is food?
Where jingles jangle your nerves?

Not for you the common muttwich, reeking
of heat, spattering fat, Happy Meals for
goofballs, wafts of fracedinous meats.

Ronald looks insane, for one thing.
It's not so much in your elite disdain
you're mortified with all your pride

cartoons have become American gods.
You don't want it known your mouth is wide,
you're urgent, resigned to get in line.

Little kids buried under snowfalls
of fries, wolfing mouthfeel, are too common
with their shouting to be loved.

You have no weakness for curious episodes,
Miss Glass-ass. No backyard vegetables for you.
You won't eat with bedouins, lesser breeds

of finch, smouts with mustard on their noses.
You want dignity, not oily fingers arrayed around
something round and wet like waferbeef.

Down with Tuna Colorado, hot as heated hands
and smelling like the dump! Vile untouchables in
booths! Suricates munching ghost crabs!

How priggishly you'd turn aside
The way royalty in rouge would sniff at oranges
processing among the benighted.

Let them pronounce ketchup in Wyoming.
You won't appear hearty for anything you eat.
A whopper through a window in a wagging fist

mocks you like a motley clown reminds you
with his foolery and fistpie face only of yourself
howling to a waiter for another drink,

clashes with your choosy charm. Your hair.
You want decor and tablecloths and violins,
opera-length pearls, a curving stair,

a dunce to dance attendance on your needs,
celebutantes, friends, walletfuls of funshine,
like movie stars in silver ogled from afar

in limousines coursing through the night
through streets of an expensive dark to Rollo's
for champagne and salmon caviar.

These blue potatoes are not *pommes
de terre dauphinoises,* nor a richly colored Merlot
that papercup of fizzing piss.

Attitudes can thrive only for a time.
Your insulting scream for us to eat hot death
Is cruel to all crumbbummery,

And fortune can reverse. Things change.
When, poor ditchwitch, fate being what it is,
you should begin to fail, to roam about,

muttering on roads in your aluminum hat
and ripped old sneakers or shoeboxes for shoes,
looking for a dog to greet,

rummaging through dirty barrels
for a rusk, no longer golden, your arches fallen,
remember well the food you snubbed.

The Spittoon Has Gone Ceramic

The spittoon has gone ceramic,
The parade ground mossy.
Once, in a midafternoon, I thought
We knew our bargains.

There's a glimp in the tear,
A crimp in my shin; I hurt
For the huge afternoons
When packs of flowers were laid at my door.

Nowhere is the lovely bassoon
That etched out funny notes at me.
The tumbling kids of my mother
Now square themselves in boxes.

In front of me my friends, the kids,
Jam their thumbs past their teeth,
And question each moment of transfiguration.
Swivel-eyed, they beware of things.

And so as I brush memories from the corner
Of my head, wait pleasantly for the needle
To slip into the groove, I fright at the
Lost big things that have made me turn on my heel.

It does no one good to fill up on bread
When the Hallowe'en children ask for meals,
Nor can one feed lovely little shadows
That tattoo glee-steps on your front door.

But when did I deny, though this was fleeting,
That this was love?
I tune my ears willingly to the corduroyed
Boy ready with his trumpet for me.

And though standing like a blue doll in my room
For the smacky knocks for candy
I cannot forget: remember my own
Thatchy hair and wide wide glimpse.

Oh yes, I have danced on the stones;
I have bounced into the bright water of the sea.
But still I watch out for myself in the rain
And wait for the link between world and toy.

The spittoon has gone ceramic,
The parade ground mossy.
Once, in a midafternoon, I thought
We knew our bargains.

The Star-Spangled Banner

The choral group from Somerville
Swaying from side to side?
The goon from the local Moose lodge
Who steps to the mike in one stride?
Irish tenors, young starlets,
DJs who claim they can sing?
On a bet from the bar the moron
Who thought he'd give it a fling?
Those VFW fascists,
Mainstays of the Sunday school choir,
Painfully sucking in air
Crazily breathing out fire?
Miss Muttjack who suddenly came to
The difficult "rockets' red glare"
And reddened just like the rockets
And virtually tore out her hair?
The Italian boy whose accordion
Wheezed like the doors of a bus?
Montes parturient;
Nascetur ridiculus mus.
The opera singer from Eboli
With pesto sauce on his breath
Made me prefer to living
An instantaneous death.
The chubby lady who howled it
Spotlit on an ice-cold rink
Who snatched at the hem of a dress
That might have been cut from zinc?
(The echo alone of her voices
As she practiced some in the hall
Sounded to me like a gang-bang
In the parking lot of a mall.)
The Negro hipster was charming
Who did it in flatted thirds,
Though he sang the "twilight's *glass* gleaming,"
And the haircut from local radio
Quickly forgot the words.
Look, no one can do the Anthem,
Whether singing it soft or loud;
A law should be passed in America:

No one should be allowed!
I'll gladly abridge one freedom
Despite what our forefathers say;
The "Land of the freeee," forget it.
And the "hooome of the braa-aave"?
No way.

Strange in My Hencoop

Strange in my hencoop
Was the frost that killed.
I waited all alive as usual
Braving off in mittens all the cold—
Translations of my body
White now in the frost.
Three friends also were alive,
Not as wordy but as nice;
They'd come to hammer on the breaded screen
To tell me of the frost,
Warning as they should
To stamp freely in the cold.
(Once, we jumped on hens.)
It had been warm once;
We had had the fun warmth brings
The days when foolhood was acceptable
As awful chickens,
Rotten in their offal, in their skulls
As blue and light as ounces.
We weren't so frost-faced then,
But positive as music in our trousers,
Firm as decency, alive as coals,
And clever in our faces, then.
We wasted time with easy persecutions,
Glad as girls with our advantage
As we stoned the chickens
And pulverized the hens,
Sticking with a passion we would never
Ever understand
Golden pins into brainless hens.
Prosperity, however, freezes;
One must know his hencoop,
Surely, to make advantage work.
I wait in the ice of my hencoop,
Feel with gloom the icy nettles
Underneath my boots,
And wait for friends, both thin and jeweled,
Deliberate as frozen,
Exclusive as I'm chilled,
Jumping to the fence with my hands,

My eyes as wide as doors, and scared,
Pouncing now on feathers and on blood.
There are no chickens now,
For they're all dead
And beaten into dust where
Strange in my hencoop
Was the frost that killed.

Tammy Wynette

I'll never forget,
Your waving at me from the stage
One hot July night
At the Barnstable County Fair.
So I forgive you your many husbands,
Don Chapel, Georges Jones and Richie,
Chaw-chewing Euple Byrd,
All those flings with other men,
You were desperate and hurt:
Why else would a woman take up with Burt?
You needed love, like as not,
Ever since you stole your first kiss
With A. G. Stepp
When you were only thirteen years old
(What I was is not what I am)
In the balcony of the movie
The-a-ter in Red Bay, Alabam.
Think of the pain of this country queen!
Gallbladder surgery, electric shock,
Kidney infections, a ruptured spleen.
(The lurid locutions of trouble and strife
Echo Ralph Edwards on *This Is Your Life*.)
How many pregnancies? Beatings as well.
Then headlines! Abduction! Another seduction?
You're given up for lost! *She's dead!*
But then you appear—
Who can explain it, no motive was clear.
("Try six kids and a country career!"
The Nashville cynics said.)
But music's about those you make glad.
There's Aunt Princie Hamby, loyal and true,
Uncle Harrod, and Hollice, your dad.
After all, it's the family that counts
And multiple marriages needn't be sad;
And who has to know this better than you?
Your mom—Ms. Mildred Faye Russell Lee Pugh!
That lonely feeling? When few seem to care?
Didn't I feel it myself,
Walking home all alone
From the Barnstable County Fair?

Hey, Tammy, you do what you can—
You stood what you could,
Even if not by your man.

Thanks for the Memory

Thanks for the memory
Of New Jersey's lovely shores
Moorestown and its bores
The piano bits you tried to play but buggered up the scores
How lovely it was!
Thanks for the memory
Of rainy afternoons
Meals with dirty spoons
Talks with you that seemed less eloquent than Icelandic runes
How lovely it was!
Many's the time you got weepy
Over your father's odd life
Your mother's sexual strife
No eschewing their wrongdoing.
And thanks for the memory
Of your brother's pompous pride
Which no one could abide
Mother Teresa would have killed him
But I took it all in stride
So thank you so much!

Thanks for the memory
Of humor not too swift
Not your biggest gift
Asking stories be repeated to which you never got the drift
How lovely it was!
Thanks for the memory
Your mathematic skill
Rarely fit the bill
But if murder's ever called for it's a perfect way to kill
How lovely it was!
Your friends I never met
Not a matter for regret
I thought caring partly sharing
But thanks for the memory
And when you got the blues
Calling me became your ruse
Yet I've had fortune cookies
With more fascinating news
I thank you so much!

Thanks for the memory
Of always being late
Your dresses out-of-date
The company you work for, the biggest polluter in the state.
How lovely it was!
Thanks for the memory
Of meals you tried to cook
Even following a book
That cassoulet you turned out tasted like a blackened rook
How lovely it was!
The sports you couldn't do
Set your jaw with bitter rue
After a year I couldn't care
Yet thanks for the memory
Of every mousy curl
Skin that felt like burl
I swear I could have whittled
A more congenial girl
But thank you so much!

(With thanks to the Paramount Music Corp. and acknowledgment of the original version, words and music by Leo Robin and Ralph Rainger © 1937.)

Three Questions

Why do grebes with a clutch
Who ask nothing of Tibet
Feed their young with feathers?
Even pundits cannot say.

Who's to blame when empty
They should fall from the sky
When they feed on what they fly,
The grebes with a clutch,

The pundits who can't say,
Or something in or of the sky
That makes them fly and fall,
From feathers they weren't fed?

Tiresias in Mushroom Town

The Honourable Stephen Tennant arrived in an electric brougham
wearing a football jersey and earrings.
                    —William Hickey, *Daily Express* (1927)

We all have the chances
              our centuries give;
    We meet with its old men and dogs,
    And the days we now see
    The women are free,
    And the men go forth in their gowns.
In the beautiful, beautiful mushroom towns,
In the beautiful mushroom towns.

We inherit with glimpses
              surrounding modes,
    The habits of our time are safe,
    Girls waddle to work,
    With a masculine shirk,
    The sweet boys continue their rounds.
In the beautiful, beautiful mushroom towns,
In the beautiful mushroom towns.

We stand mute and accept
              the available times,
    Never letting the question arise:
    Is a man somehow less,
    If he's wearing a dress,
    Or weeping when watching a clown.
In the beautiful, beautiful mushroom towns,
In the beautiful mushroom towns.

To R. J.

Because your eyes light up what in
My life makes spring of what's begun
The warmth you give creates a dream within
And so till now I have not seen the sun.

Because that light like sun creates in bliss
A passion warmest seasons fail to bring
It wakens dreams where lovers always kiss
And so till now I have not seen the spring.

To the Eight American Women Soldiers
Slain in Vietnam

How you went involves
No longer why you came,
But that you did,
Ten thousand strong,
And by those dying men
Who lost their lives
You added yours.
There were eight of you.
A memorial now stands
Along the Washington mall,
Name upon numberless name.
A sadness comes in reading
Anyone's name on a wall.
A sharper pain is felt
Among them finding you.
Can anyone explain?
Could it be that you so few
Who were so brave
Intensify the pain?

For Eleanor Alexander
Pamela Donovan
Carol Drazba
Annie Graham
Elizabeth Jones
Mary Klinker
Sharon Lane
Hedwig Orlowski

Turkana Girl

Sweet black pharoah,
With your finely
Chiseled face
And graceful nose
Flatly shaped
For looking down,
Milk your camels
In Nadikam
Without a sound.
In moonlight
Toying slyly with your beads,
Flirting with me
Up and down
You slide your hand
Along their leads.
I dream of you
Moaning *ululu, ululu.*
Whip me with your rat-tail hair,
Goddess, dressed, unlike you,
Naked, hot as Kenya,
Open legs in passion,
With the mixture of fat
And black earth
Out of which,
Girl of the dark,
I choose to think
That you, like
The shadows of
Your dreams,
Are fashioned.

TV News in America

An empty cab pulled up in front of 10 Downing Street and out
stepped Clement Atlee.

—Winston Churchill

Don't be fooled:
The trick is
To tell them
What you've told them
And then show them
What they have to see
To be told.
("He just ran for a touchdown,"
Howard Cosell said,
Who looks like an insect
With earphones on his head,
But that handoff, that long run,
Hadn't we just seen
The *ana* and *katabasis*
In the picture on the screen?)
Stupid is in,
Not out,
Dollars in accounts
Receivable, no doubt.
War is ratings,
(Not on the battlefield)
Emotions only aped.
Sex, death, violence.
("How did you feel
When your daughter was raped?")
That bite, maybe we can
Add an ad, you know
To show with it?
Go with it.

Vinyl Junkie

What did
Gaynel Hodge and the Turks
Who sang "Fathertime" (Keen)
So great
Know in 1958
That made them so fine?
Or the Pearls
With "Jungle Bunny" (Dooto)
Back in 1959?
The Five Thrills on Parrot,
The Clovers on Atlantic,
First gave me a picture
Of white girls frantic.
What first moved my soul?
A dance, a deck of smokes,
The Harptones'
"Sunday Kind of Love" (Bruce),
My hair in a roll.
The Olympics, the Penguins,
The Acrobatics,
Little Augie Austin and the Chromatics,
Chubby and the Turnpikes,
What satisfaction!
Throw in Zodiac Mindwarp
And the Love Reaction.
I want you to know
For what you went through,
Practicing wage slaves,
Old auditoriums, drafty halls,
Broken contracts, unanswered calls
To teach me
Love was bop,
You reached me.
Doo wop.

The Way to Cedar Rapids

1

What Cedar Rapids waits
For you depends on who you are
And what you want.

2

Imagining the way
That Cedar Rapids is
Is not to have to go.

3

Not to have to go
To Cedar Rapids and being there
Is much the same.

4

Among the more irritating
Ideas are that those who go
Whistling off to Cedar Rapids,
like small retailing Nebuchadunsaw
With his train schedules,
Grow large.

5

Do you have to know
By white anemic maps the way
Others go to Cedar Rapids and return
With rodomontades?

6

A better way to know
Cedar Rapids is often not to go,
As if going there mattered
More than not.

7

Two plus two equals four
Discovers exactly nothing
Only restates it, megadick,
Even in blessedly feathery Cedar Rapids.

You have not seen a city or a soul,
Neither transfigure nor adopt,
Only verify.

8

In your dreams
The way to Cedar Rapids
Is not the way to go.

9

What would you co-opt
When you take out your loupe?
Cedar Rapids is a pratfall of facts
No more than someone who makes a wish
Scorning necessary acts
Necessarily is.

10

Nor is to go to Cedar Rapids
The way to know, no more the source
Than the solution of whatever attributes
Beautiful fancy feeds us.
Are we the world we walk on?

11

Only in the mind
Can we tell Cedar Rapids
How when we've been there or never been
We're never wholly through with
What we've seen.

12

In real Cedar Rapids
A spirit that is stricken
Makes the bones dry, too. My gaze
Is for that grace unaware of itself,
Imagining pale alexandrites,
Say, in skylight.

Welsh Englyn

A good englyn must have four lines, of ten, then six, syllables, the last two lines having seven syllables each. The first two lines are called the *Toddaid Byr,* the second two the *cywydd* stanza. In the first line there must be a break after the seventh, eighth, or ninth syllable, a detached section called the *gair cyrch,* which may consist of one, two, or three syllables, and the rhyme with the second line comes at this break; but the tenth syllable of the first line must either rhyme or be in assonance with the middle of the second line. The last two lines must rhyme with the first rhyme in the first line, but the third or fourth line must rhyme on a weak syllable. The englyn is an ancient verse form that originated from Welsh imitations of the Latin epitaphs on the gravestones of the Britons.

In foul New Haven sits a school—called Yale,
   Beyond the pale and cruel;
W ant to learn to be a fool
In a place to ridicule?

Then to Connecticut please come—make haste,
   Be two-faced, even dumb;
The general faculty here is scum
All winter, spring, and autumn.

When the Circumcision Screams Die Down

When the circumcision screams die down,
The gingerbread licks quickly off the finger.
Remember the attic with its shadows
And the boards that smelled like Christmas
Where we slept in rows like elves?
I had for play a riddle of a rattle
And let the monkey with the plastic face,
Furrowed like sweet old granny's shank,
Squirm in beside my knee—you know,
The small fur thing I kept nearby
For safety's sake? We jabbered late
After being read to in our trundles
And twirled for fun the radio dials,
Upsetting dear ol' Dad and toasty Mom,
Who kissed us covered in our bunting,
Where I felt safe in my short bed,
My thumb locked on my monkey friend,
A peppery little gnome between
My dreams and that dark wall I saw
And studied when I couldn't sleep
For joy, the moonlight in my face.
I wonder was I any less a fairy tale
Than what I dreamt of when I wished?
Every wondrous thing that I imagined
I waited hopefully to see come true.
I'm sure I blundered as I slept,
Lost beneath blankets and pink puffs
After hearing stories in the night
To find them echo in my dreams,
Reverberating everywhere it seemed
But when I awoke to morning light.
Of what we never had we knew, yet
Heard so many tales we never cried,
But when we crack open the rattle,
What is left a person but to stare
Outraged and bewildered and sad
At the tiny bead inside?

When You're Looking with Your Right Eye

> I thank you with all my heart for your gallant generosity in writing
> to me of that which I've longed not to lose the so terribly twisted
> clue to.
>
> —Henry James

When you're looking with your right eye,
Your left eye isn't there.
I watch the elephant in girls,
Alone and masticating treacle in the movies,
But they become Snow White and tenderness
When I turn and watch the gum machine
Kicked and rolled about by floozies,
Bold in their nylons and plumpy in their dress
And smirking funny in their swatches of hair
Because when you're looking with your right eye,
Your left eye isn't there.
Appendicitis hurts; it's bad.
But it's moonlight and balloons you say
When that baby's in the groin,
The upshot of your hubby's play.
Though he's able to paint on Saturday morns
The whole of your house and its dome,
Weeping and blinking in his underwear fumes,
Your freaky son mopes home:
Six feet in the second grade, far too much he grew.
Yes, right wrongs in the librarian's eyes
When the book, all right on a Friday night,
On Saturday is overdue.
Some call meat a flank and some a loin;
My granny may call some things false;
My grampy maybe true.
At once a woman becomes a whore
When her goofy partner, through,
Whistles happy out the door and leaves behind a coin.
Some say it's an ogle and some say it's a stare
When you look with all your might;
But let's forget my granny and ask a question here:
When you're looking with your left eye,
Then what about the right?

Who Isn't What

For Dale

A woman's properly beautiful
Only if something she does
Adds up to something worthy—
It's not simply someone she was
Or is, as if heaven-sent.
Why insist on maintaining
That beauty obviates training?
Worth means accomplishment.
You find it hard to agree?
Then why not expect a petunia
To assume the role of a tree?
Nelly Ternan, a mistress,
Being what she was,
Simply never became what she wasn't;
She was what she was *because.*
She was born, had great beauty,
Painted her face, wanted fame;
Why discuss what she wasn't?
Fucking was mainly her game.
She wasn't a surgeon general;
So, tell me, what else is new?
Is it so complicated
To see what we are's what we do?
No better example emerges
In spite of feminist dread
Of the Christian exhortation,
"Let the dead bury the dead."
Nell merely proceeded by choices
As dust comes only to dust
And hung herself
As an ornament
(Ignoring Victorian voices)
On Mr. Dickens's lust.

A Widgin of a Thing with a Face Like a Gun

A widgin of a thing with a face like a gun,
    her nose between the glass and her idea for blood,
    was sent home by her son on Christmas.

After the airport, bumping through the air made blood
    fluster to her neck, bitten like the tree of Christmas,
    holding her cream cup, she wanted no umbrella but a gun.

Sonny didn't care, the foul ball who peed on Christmas
    many a night, and wasn't ready for cracky hugs or blood
    relations, now—a man who knew nothing of the gun.

Winterreise

Remember at the beach the sun,
The funfare, bumping cars, lights,
Penny arcades, shooting galleries
And the machine with the Gypsy woman
Who spit out your fortune on a card,
The big head of a laughing clown,
Going Ho-ho-ho? How far we walked.
At one point we got lost. And scared.
It was gray at the end of the esplanade.
The wind came up. And it grew cold.
We could no longer smell the beach.
In a dirty parking lot filled with broken
Glass, an empty oil drum, I sat
And waited for a long, long time.
I knew what Dad would have said,
"There are no more rides." Now he's dead.
So's Mom. And you were everybody.

Winter Wounds

Imagine the moron
Who is loved
Thinking she deserves
By looks or fame or fate
Another's heart,
And so reserves
Part of what she thinks
She shouldn't give
To her less-deserving mate.
You can take the time,
Queen Pig, to spend
A lifetime as a fop?
We deserve nothing,
Unless everything—
You are certainly
Not enough—
To compensate for all
The lies we're told,
Your haughty huffs.
If someone in the world
Should ever be chosen
To rage against the cold
At the last minute,
The pall of coming death,
It won't be me;
I'll welcome it,
Without deliberation,
Without a reservation,
Winter wounds and all.

Wittgenstein's Proposal

After two weeks she [Marguerite Respinger] left for Rome to attend her sister's wedding, determined that the one man she was *not* going to marry was Ludwig Wittgenstein.

—Ray Monk, *Ludwig Wittgenstein*

For me
As I hope for you
Discovering a sentence
Has no means
Of verification
Is to understand
Something important
About it
But not to discover
That there is nothing in it
To understand.
Will you
Give me your hand?

The World as Will and Idea

1

You have a name
Before you even scream
Carried on your head
As heavy as the leaden years,
Tumble into playgrounds
Where someone waits to beat you up
Because of your squint,
Wide ears, or folded lunches.
It's all been there before,
All the news,
Tired old proverbs, old debates.
Face, feet, desperate hunches.
What in life isn't thrown at you
Like clothes?
How many Christmases
Happily took place
Before you had a chance to be?
We receive our lives
Like broken sets of plates
For six, except we're one.
We inherit all we have.
If nothing is new,
Even worse
Nothing more awaits
Under the sun.

2

I hate the world
For what in being what it is
It isn't. The wet, the wind,
Vacant yards, broken gates,
Fistfights, not enough light,
Man both debt and debtor,
Animals, weeping, locked in pens,
You couldn't imagine better?
What, waiting lifetimes for a tender kiss?
Who with any brains
That can't foresee a better world
Could be satisfied with this?

Face it, there *isn't* any truth.
We're no more preconceived
Than if our fathers at a fun fair
Plopped a coin in a machine
And out bonked a Baby Ruth.
History makes of teachers
Something obscene.
I look at piles
Of ragged sheet music
Fifty years old
And think: *dead people,*
Names in the night,
All gone, basically sold.

3

We're born against our will
And die the same,
Depend by strictly chance
Upon the wife we meet,
Fail to succeed for her,
But still must take the blame.
This is the way
You say it has to be?
Raving half-mad prophets
Running quaquaversal
Throughout the streets,
Drooling hobo harridans
In dirty doorways curled,
Two-thirds of a population
Revolving in a starving world?
I prefer to be told
We find our fate, our fortune,
In the street.
We all are tempted
By our dreams
Of what could be,
The way they come,
But it's only the daring
The brave, the truthful,
Who succumb.

Yale

Look down, Elihu, we're all right,
Still echoes your boola blue chorus:
Faculty women have faces like night,
Professors go mincing like florists,
Padlocks on buildings, empty graces,
Shallow youth with missing faces.
The colleges rise like broken rocks.
Its stone like frozen sleet is cold.
The tower thrust of Harkness mocks
The eunuchs who in classrooms old
Twist literature of noble breadth
Into verbal games, like living death.
I pray heaven's azure is a different hue
Than Yale's, asphyxiation's ghastly blue.

Zucchini

On the morgue floor lay
Paul Castellano, murdered

mobster who, being impotent,
had had a gooseneck lamp

implant some years before
a rival gang shut the door.

An oddity in someone shot,
paradoxically so,

Little Pauly was ready to go
Big Pauly was not.

Index of First Lines

A la saison des Nobels, au printemps   13
"After the lovin' "   74
All the boys knew Mary Snowfire   96
Almost old as powdered white   52
As a literary agent   121
As reasonable as muffins   62
Autumnal days make me believe   70
A very thin premeditated ghost   45
A widgin of a thing with a face like a gun   160
A woman's properly beautiful   159
Because your eyes light up what in   149
Black flags, black rags   49
Blackwind kneels in silence all alone   16
Bowls of snibbled beans   25
Buried in a yell is something from the throat   65
But you won't be seen there   135
By the waters now of doom I sit   23
Celebrate, America, and crow   115
Christmas dinner had melon for dessert   32
"Circle" Burke was a nasty piece of work   34
Deception is the price too many pay for love   73
Does the poetry of women lie   59
Don't be fooled   152
Don't they find their faces hatchets   132
Do the high violins of your Symphony no. 1   21
Dr. Nathan Pritikin   100
Everyone's fat friend is first to coo   55
Fasting makes a face that lights an onion up   103
Fiction's fun to feign. It mutters up the sleeve   57
For all the violence men create   48
For me   163
Found nowhere in the Bible   11
Fr. Mario used to visit our house   60
Gravures are kisses   36
Grow, lovely child   124
Hand me my populuxe hat   74
He combed his hair, proud   97
How can a sex   125
How find joy enough to survive   7
How you went involves   150
I am fat with vision   113
I'd never seen you   22
"I don't *do* blurbs!" you screech   116
I fear my name   2

If love is the licking and tugs at the movies   76
If on a friend's bookshelf   123
I have a certain sympathy with war   117
I'll never forget   143
Imagine the moron   162
I'm a nightstick man, gone canoninize yo bitch   17
In foul New Haven sits a school—called Yale   156
In quiet Amherst   54
In the children's parks is fun   81
I poked about for friends in winter   128
I remember, I remember still   95
I searched for you in Critical, Mass.   91
I think of death at times   75
It was cracked like a Weetabix   12
It wasn't him   51
I've always loved your smile   3
La neige, c'est cette tige étrange que l'on coupe a l'été   56
Like a novel, like a sequel   71
Look down, Elihu, we're all right   166
Love, O what if in my dreaming wild   50
Matsu, spread out your netsukes   87
Miss Amy Lowell was butch   19
Moses murdered a man, flat out   105
Most compound consonantal sounds   134
Most of him recalled for me   90
Nobody could love you   83
Once my god we allow for accusations   107
On the morgue floor lay   167
On the reservation   6
O red-wigged wit from Tambov   104
O Swung Tree   68
Part of loving's leaving   114
Pressant   84
Remember at the beach the sun   161
"She's really not a bad sort"   108
Shoot it, baby   35
Spare me the girl whose best friend is her mother   43
Squinting into the sun   86
Strange in my hencoop   141
Sweet black pharaoh   151
Take those Dadaists with frying pans   85
Thanks for the memory   145
The choral group from Somerville   139
The chunky little men turn red   118
The girl who makes you cry is always love   63
The meeting of the heads with eyes   98

The new soft bells tune in anew   122
The only way   93
There were cobblers, cocktails, white cups, and flips   111
The spittoon has gone ceramic   137
The steeple clock marks half-past twelve   30
Twice within the week so given   126
We all have the chances our centuries give   148
We all heard the mad birds   78
Were you ever an altar boy   38
What Cedar Rapids waits   154
What cook who makes a poisoned pie   24
What did   153
What head isn't filled with feathers   15
What is the secret said   102
What I thought   79
What polishes, like gold   9
What, sculptor, do you see   130
What would you do   80
When Charlene Pigg reads the news   133
When I take God upstairs   64
When the circumcision screams die down   157
When we take her upstairs in the attic   1
When you're looking with your right eye   158
When you touch me, there is silver up my back   37
Where are the truths you wanted to hear   82
Who makes a kind of crowing, clacks its teeth at birds   28
Why cut your braids   101
Why do grebes with a clutch   147
With his pistols   120
Would the girl I took to see   41
You have a name   164
You loved to strut   109
You might think perhaps that a bully   131
Young Henry McCarty roamed the Lower East Side   14
Your alias might have been   29
Your eyes please keep   58
"Your themocouple's broke"   99
You stand, old school, bright upon a hill   5
You were both death on a bun   53
You were not brought up on A Street   18

This first edition of *The Lollipop Trollops and Other Poems* is published in both paperback and hardback editions. Of the latter, 100 copies have been signed and numbered by the author and by the cover designer. Numbers 1-50 are for sale, and 51-100 are *hors de commerce,* reserved for the use of the author and illustrator.

No. _____/100